Contents

Acknowledgments

This resource was originally developed and pilot tested by the Children First initiative in St. Louis Park, Minnesota. This community initiative has generously shared this material with Search Institute and with other individuals, organizations, and communities that seek to encourage and equip individuals to make personal commitments to asset building.

Formed in 1993, Children First was the first community-wide initiative organized to build the developmental assets identified by Search Institute. In 1996, Children First began a concerted effort to bring asset building into individual neighborhoods within the city. This resource was developed as a tool for that effort.

Taking Asset Building Personally was first developed by Children First's Neighborhood Task Force as a way to encourage residents to integrate asset building into their personal lives. Thanks to all the members of the Neighborhood Discussion Guide Task Force who helped conceptualize this resource. They were Karen Atkinson, Susan Farr, Bridget Gothberg, Charlie Meyers, Bob Ramsey, Eugene Roehlkepartain, Jolene Roehlkepartain, Terri Sullivan, and Bob Wittman (who wrote the Guide for Planning and Facilitating Study Groups and facilitated the pilot group).

In addition, the tool was pilot tested with a group of community residents in St. Louis Park. Thanks to the participants, who not only faithfully attended sessions, but offered thoughtful feedback that informed the final shape of this resource: Ellen Becher, Sara Bjelde, Todd Looney, Bob Polland, Sue Santa, Serena Steffenhagen, Ashley Tomoson, and Don Turkington.

In addition, we thank the following people who reviewed this resource to ensure its usefulness in many settings and groups across the United States: Ellen Albee, Nancy Ashley, Karen Atkinson, Carol Breslau, Joy DesMarais, Marilyn Erickson, Holly Halvorson, Rick Jackson, Darrel Peterson, Derek Peterson, Flora Sanchez, Virginia Soberg, Terri Sullivan, Terri Swanson, and Bob Wittman.

Finally, we thank the people on Search Institute's editorial team who prepared this resource for publication: Ann Betz, Kalisha Davis, Dyanne Drake, Jeannie Ford, Jennifer Griffin-Wiesner, Kathryn (Kay) L. Hong, Sandy Longfellow, Karen Pladsen, Eugene C. Roehlkepartain, and Amanda Seigel.

Introduction

Today's children and teenagers need you in their lives. You have much to offer young people, whether you're a teenager, a parent, a neighbor, a grandparent, an empty nester, a single adult, or a senior citizen.

What can you do for young people? You can build their "developmental assets"—40 building blocks that are essential for young people's successful growth and development. Identified by Search Institute through extensive research on children and youth, these 40 assets represent positive experiences, opportunities, and relationships that all young people need from the time they're born until they are adults.

You don't have to have special training to build these assets (which are explained in more detail in Chapter 1). You don't have to be a parent, teacher, or other professional. You just need to be someone who cares about kids and who is willing to take a few extra steps to help them grow up healthy, caring, and responsible.

The Purpose of *Taking Asset Building Personally*

This workbook helps you discover ways you can build assets for children and youth and grow in your personal commitment to make a difference in the lives of young people. *Taking Asset Building Personally: An Action and Reflection Workbook* helps you:

- Understand and remember basic information about the eight categories of developmental assets;
- Examine your personal responsibility, ability, and opportunities to build assets;
- Develop new skills that will help you be more comfortable and effective in building assets; and
- Commit to specific ways you will build assets for young people in your nuclear or extended family, school, neighborhood, organization, or community.

Chances are you already do things right now that build assets. This work will help you see this and point you in the direction of doing asset building intentionally.

How This Workbook Is Organized

This workbook begins by introducing the 40 assets and general ways you can—and do—build them. Then there are chapters to help you understand and reflect upon each of the eight categories of developmental assets. Each chapter includes:

- A brief introduction to the category of assets along with ideas for building them with and for children and youth; and
- Several easy-to-use worksheets and questions that help you think about how you build these assets.

A concluding chapter then ties all the pieces together. That chapter is followed by a listing of other resources for additional study on each asset.

We realize this is a lot to think about and try out. Keep in mind that you can always revisit this workbook, so it's not necessary to know, be, and do everything right away or all the time. Take simple steps and keep building.

Putting Children First

Many communities across the United States are working together with new energy and inspiration to create a more positive future for their children and teenagers, using the 40 assets as their launching pad. In Georgetown, Texas, where utility workers are trained in asset building, service trucks bear "A Safe Place" logo so that young people in an emergency can spot help quickly. A Newark, Ohio, judge has introduced asset building to more than 600 juvenile offenders and paired them with caring mentors and community service. And in Kodiak, Alaska, public health nurses talk to parents about the power of assets during well-child exams.

But no matter how much community action occurs or how many organizations make official commitments to asset building, the efforts will be incomplete unless individuals—people of all ages and from all walks of life—make personal commitments to spend time with, guide, support, and care for children and teenagers in new ways.

At its core, this is what asset building is all about: people taking this role personally and deciding to make changes in their own lives that put young people first. Asset building doesn't have to be complicated or expensive. It doesn't even have to take a lot of extra time. But asset building may be one of the best investments you'll ever make. Enjoy the journey!

Using This Workbook with Small Groups

While you can use this guide on your own for personal reflection and study, the ideal way to work through it is with a small group of people who can share experiences and ideas and support each other in asset building.

If you're part of a discussion group that is using this guide, you'll complete some of the pages during the group sessions. Others will be assigned as homework for the next session. Some pages may not be directly addressed during the sessions. They are for your own reference.

If you want to engage others in a conversation about asset building, a group planning and facilitators guide is available from Search Institute. The companion guide, *Taking Asset Building Personally: A Guide for Planning and Facilitating Study Groups,* gives ideas for setting up discussion groups in your community or organization, and it offers step-by-step instructions for leading six 90-minute discussions.

CHAPTER 1

Everyone's an Asset Builder

Why do some young people grow up with ease, while others struggle? Why do some youth get involved in dangerous activities, while others spend their time contributing to society in positive ways? Why do some youth "beat the odds" in difficult situations, while others get trapped?

Many factors shape young people's lives and choices—economic circumstances, family dynamics, genetics, traumatic events. Research by Search Institute has identified 40 concrete, positive experiences and qualities—called *developmental assets*—that have a tremendous influence on young people's lives. The assets (listed on page 2) are grouped in eight categories.

The 40 developmental assets represent everyday wisdom about positive experiences young people need. These assets help make it less likely that young people will get involved in problem behaviors. They also make it more likely that young people will engage in positive behaviors. This power is evident across all cultural and socioeconomic groups of youth. In Mesa, Arizona, for example, young aerosol muralists once headed for trouble are building their own assets by turning their street-wise talent into works of art for their school and community. In a rural Iowa community, 20 juniors and seniors have created a theater presentation called "We're Not Buying It" to address such topics as smoking, alcohol abuse, and low self-esteem. In St. Charles, Minnesota, mentoring has helped a 14-year-old Laotian boy who speaks English as a second language contribute weekly columns to the community newspaper. And, in Washington, D.C., two Latino teenagers have created bilingual workbooks and audiotapes that encourage immigrant families and their children to preserve Spanish skills, build English proficiency, and enjoy time together.

While the assets are powerful in shaping young people's lives and choices, too few young people experience enough of these assets. According to Search Institute research with nearly 100,000 6th- to 12th-grade youth, the average young person surveyed experiences only 18 of the 40 assets. Indeed, 20 of the 40 assets are experienced by fewer than half of youth.

Building a foundation of assets for all children and teenagers may be the most critical challenge—and opportunity—facing our society. This building begins as indi-

What Are Developmental Assets?

Essential building blocks for young people's successful growth and development.

The Eight Categories of Developmental Assets

1 **Support**—Young people need to experience support, care, and love from their families and many others. They need organizations and institutions that provide positive, supportive environments.

2 **Empowerment**—Young people need to be valued by their community and have opportunities to contribute to others. For this to occur, they must be safe and feel secure.

3 **Boundaries and Expectations**—Young people need to know what is expected of them and whether activities and behaviors are "in bounds" or "out of bounds."

4 **Constructive Use of Time**—Young people need constructive, enriching opportunities for growth through creative activities, youth programs, congregational involvement, and quality time at home.

5 **Commitment to Learning**—Young people need to develop a lifelong commitment to education and learning.

6 **Positive Values**—Youth need to develop strong values that guide their choices.

7 **Social Competencies**—Young people need skills and competencies that equip them to make positive choices, to build relationships, and to succeed in life.

8 **Positive Identity**—Young people need a strong sense of their own power, purpose, worth, and promise.

viduals choose to treat young people differently and put their well-being above all else. Getting personally involved in asset building and encouraging others to do the same is one of the most important commitments you can make for the future of young people and our society.

40 Developmental Assets

**Search Institute has identified the following building blocks of healthy development
that help young people grow up healthy, caring, and responsible.**

EXTERNAL ASSETS

Support

1. **Family support**—Family life provides high levels of love and support.
2. **Positive family communication**—Young person and her or his parent(s) communicate positively, and young person is willing to seek advice and counsel from parent(s).
3. **Other adult relationships**—Young person receives support from three or more nonparent adults.
4. **Caring neighborhood**—Young person experiences caring neighbors.
5. **Caring school climate**—School provides a caring, encouraging environment.
6. **Parent involvement in schooling**—Parent(s) are actively involved in helping young person succeed in school.

Empowerment

7. **Community values youth**—Young person perceives that adults in the community value youth.
8. **Youth as resources**—Young people are given useful roles in the community.
9. **Service to others**—Young person serves in the community one hour or more per week.
10. **Safety**—Young person feels safe at home, at school, and in the neighborhood.

Boundaries & Expectations

11. **Family boundaries**—Family has clear rules and consequences and monitors the young person's whereabouts.
12. **School boundaries**—School provides clear rules and consequences.
13. **Neighborhood boundaries**—Neighbors take responsibility for monitoring young people's behavior.
14. **Adult role models**—Parent(s) and other adults model positive, responsible behavior.
15. **Positive peer influence**—Young person's best friends model responsible behavior.
16. **High expectations**—Both parent(s) and teachers encourage the young person to do well.

Constructive Use of Time

17. **Creative activities**—Young person spends three or more hours per week in lessons or practice in music, theater, or other arts.
18. **Youth programs**—Young person spends three or more hours per week in sports, clubs, or organizations at school and/or in the community.
19. **Religious community**—Young person spends one or more hours per week in activities in a religious institution.
20. **Time at home**—Young person is out with friends "with nothing special to do" two or fewer nights per week.

INTERNAL ASSETS

Commitment to Learning

21. **Achievement motivation**—Young person is motivated to do well in school.
22. **School engagement**—Young person is actively engaged in learning.
23. **Homework**—Young person reports doing at least one hour of homework every school day.
24. **Bonding to school**—Young person cares about her or his school.
25. **Reading for pleasure**—Young person reads for pleasure three or more hours per week.

Positive Values

26. **Caring**—Young person places high value on helping other people.
27. **Equality and social justice**—Young person places high value on promoting equality and reducing hunger and poverty.
28. **Integrity**—Young person acts on convictions and stands up for her or his beliefs.
29. **Honesty**—Young person "tells the truth even when it is not easy."
30. **Responsibility**—Young person accepts and takes personal responsibility.
31. **Restraint**—Young person believes it is important not to be sexually active or to use alcohol or other drugs.

Social Competencies

32. **Planning and decision making**—Young person knows how to plan ahead and make choices.
33. **Interpersonal competence**—Young person has empathy, sensitivity, and friendship skills.
34. **Cultural competence**—Young person has knowledge of and comfort with people of different cultural/racial/ethnic backgrounds.
35. **Resistance skills**—Young person can resist negative peer pressure and dangerous situations.
36. **Peaceful conflict resolution**—Young person seeks to resolve conflict nonviolently.

Positive Identity

37. **Personal power**—Young person feels he or she has control over "things that happen to me."
38. **Self-esteem**—Young person reports having a high self-esteem.
39. **Sense of purpose**—Young person reports that "my life has a purpose."
40. **Positive view of personal future**—Young person is optimistic about her or his personal future.

Everyone's an Asset Builder

FAST FACTS

Assets Make a Difference

The More Assets Young People Have, the Better

Assets have a powerful, positive effect on a young person. Assets promote actions (also called thriving behaviors) that we hope for:

- Succeeding in school.
- Helping others.
- Valuing diversity.
- Maintaining good health.
- Exhibiting leadership.
- Resisting danger.
- Delaying gratification.
- Overcoming adversity.

We know that the 40 assets also protect young people from making dangerous choices. Search Institute's research consistently shows that young people with more assets are less likely to engage in risky behaviors. In fact, researchers looked at 24 high-risk behaviors and found that young people with fewer than 10 assets are likely to get involved in 10 of these behaviors, whereas young people with 31 or more assets tend to get involved in only one.

The more assets a young person has, the *less* likely he or she is to:

- Use alcohol.
- Binge drink.
- Smoke.
- Use smokeless tobacco.
- Use inhalants.
- Use marijuana.
- Use other illicit drugs.
- Drink and drive while under the influence.
- Ride with a driver who is intoxicated.
- Have sexual intercourse.
- Shoplift.
- Vandalize.
- Get into trouble with the police.
- Hit someone.
- Hurt someone.
- Use a weapon.
- Participate in group fighting.
- Carry a weapon for protection.
- Threaten to physically harm someone.
- Skip school.
- Gamble.
- Develop an eating disorder.
- Become depressed.
- Attempt suicide.

? Did You Know?

- Positive view of personal future (asset #40) is the most common asset. Seventy percent of young people surveyed report having it.

- Creative activities (asset #17) is the least common asset. Only 19 percent of youth report having it.

Most Young People Don't Have Enough Assets

Based on Search Institute's survey of nearly 100,000 6th- to 12th-grade students, these are the percentages of youth who report each level of assets:

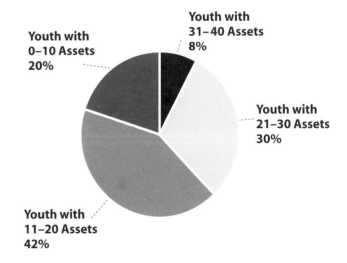

Youth with 31–40 Assets 8%

Youth with 0–10 Assets 20%

Youth with 21–30 Assets 30%

Youth with 11–20 Assets 42%

All Young People Need Assets

Although Search Institute's research on assets focuses primarily on young people in grades 6 to 12, all children need assets from day one. Here are a few ideas for building assets for children and youth at different ages. We've left spaces for you to jot down other ideas you think of or hear about.

Birth to Age 5

- Tell parents of infants about assets.
- Make a big deal when a child is born. Celebrate.
- Show parents your support. Run an errand. Offer to baby-sit.
- Sing, talk to, and play with an infant every chance you get.
- Smile and say "hi" to young children whenever you see them. Call them by name.

- _____
  _____
- _____
  _____

Ages 6 to 11

- Write a sidewalk message in chalk to a child, offering encouragement on the first day of school.
- Attend a school event, recital, concert, or sporting event of a neighborhood child.
- Greet children and take time to chat about school, movies, books, music, news, or neighborhood happenings.
- If you're a parent, invite other adults into your children's lives.

- _____
  _____
- _____
  _____

Ages 12 to 18

- Always say "hi" to teenagers and greet them by name. Continue to do this even if certain young people never respond.
- Ask young people about their favorite music group. Say you want to hear one song they especially like. Share the music you like.
- Ask youth how they build assets and how they would like assets built with and for them.
- Be intentional about building a relationship with a teenager you already know but don't know well. Spend time together doing things you both like. Find out what's important to her or him and talk about what's important to you.
- If you're a teen, reach out to someone who doesn't seem to have many friends. Send a birthday card. Celebrate even small successes.

- _____
  _____
- _____
  _____

> *"Whoever you are, there is someone younger who thinks you are perfect. There is some job that will go undone if you don't do it. There is someone who would miss you if you were gone. There is a space that you alone can fill."*
> Jacob Brande

How Asset Builders Shaped Your Life

Even though the list of 40 assets was just created in recent years, we all have experienced asset builders in our lives, whether we're age 10 or 50. In the spaces below, jot down the names of people who have built each type of asset for you and how that person has made a difference in your life.

If you are younger than 20, you may want to think about people who currently build assets for you. If you're older than 20, either think about someone who does now or think back to your own childhood and adolescence. It's okay to leave some boxes blank if no one comes to mind. It's also okay to list the same person in several boxes.

Think of someone who has . . .

Shown you love and understanding during a time when you really needed it. (Support Assets)

Helped you feel like you have something important to contribute to others. (Empowerment Assets)

Set clear boundaries for you even when it wasn't the easy thing to do. (Boundaries-and-Expectations Assets)

Helped you get a lot out of activities in your school, a youth organization, or a congregation. (Constructive-Use-of-Time Assets)

Helped you really get excited about learning new things. (Commitment-to-Learning Assets)

Been a role model in living out positive values such as honesty, integrity, and caring. (Positive-Values Assets)

Helped you develop important skills, such as getting along with other people. (Social-Competencies Assets)

Helped you feel good about yourself and optimistic about your future. (Positive-Identity Assets)

EXPLORING IDEAS

Ways You Can Build Assets

No doubt you'll have many ideas of ways to build assets once you start thinking about asset building in your life. Here are a few that others have tried and found helpful. We've also left some places for you to write in ideas that come to you.

Where You Live

- Post the list of the 40 assets on the refrigerator or some other visible place in your home. Periodically talk with friends and family about how you're doing in building the assets.
- If you live alone, eat at least one meal with friends or family each week. If others live with you, eat at least one meal together every day. Take time to talk about what's going on in each other's lives.
- Think of people who make a big difference in the lives of children. Send them each a thank-you note.

- _____
  _____
- _____
  _____

In an Organization

- Educate others in the organization—and those the organization serves—about their potential as asset builders.
- Encourage leaders to develop policies that support asset building, such as supporting youth leadership or employee volunteering.

- _____
  _____
- _____
  _____

In Your Neighborhood

- Get to know the names of children and young people who live around you. Find out what interests them. Take time to play or goof around with them.
- Treat young people with the same respect and courtesy you show to other neighbors; expect them to treat you with respect and courtesy, too.

- _____
  _____
- _____
  _____

Everyone's an Asset Builder

What Do You Hope For?

This first chapter has introduced you to the developmental assets and to the opportunities you have in your life for building these assets within the lives of young people. Where do you hope this discovery process will take you? What excites you the most? What worries you? What questions do you have?

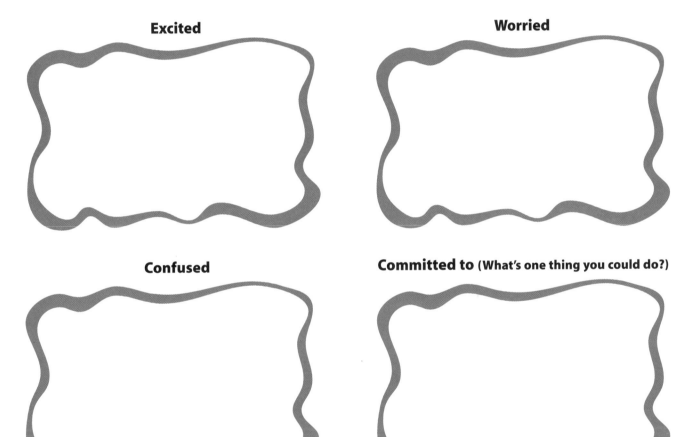

Excited

Worried

Confused

Committed to (What's one thing you could do?)

Everyday Asset Building

In the Brainerd neighborhood of Chattanooga, Tennessee, Jeannie Hall thought it would be good for neighbors to connect and get to know each other. After creating a neighborhood group and brainstorming ideas, the neighborhood now has an annual holiday celebration at the end of the year and a Fourth of July picnic. Neighbors let each other know when someone new moves into the neighborhood, about someone giving birth, or about those who need some kind of help.

When a 78-year-old woman didn't attend the Fourth of July picnic, one person took her a plate of food. Hall checked on the woman later that evening and was told that *several* people had called. People in the neighborhood watch out for each other to make sure no one feels isolated.

CHAPTER 2

Creating Caring Relationships

Support is important for everyone, young or older. We like knowing who will be there for us and whom we can count on. We enjoy the company of those who make us laugh, who make us think, who help us sort through tough issues. Support is not only the glue that holds people together but also the glue that keeps us together on the inside.

Yet, in a hectic society with so many demands, we sometimes forget the importance of noticing and connecting with one another. The result is that too many young people (and adults) feel isolated and alone.

The framework of 40 developmental assets includes six support assets that have a great impact on the way young people grow up. While most people understand the important role that families have in supporting young people, some overlook the positive power of friends, neighbors, teachers, coaches, volunteers, grandparents, bus drivers, baby-sitters, aunts and uncles, store clerks, and other people who are part of children's and teenagers' lives.

Even simple actions and gestures can help to create an atmosphere of support. After hearing about assets, for example, the owner of a grocery store in New Jersey converted a few checkout lanes, replacing tabloids and candy with educational toys and healthy snacks, to support customers with children.

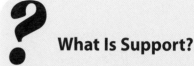

What Is Support?

Young people need to experience the presence, care, help, and love of their families and many others. They need organizations and institutions that provide positive, nurturing environments.

The Six Support Assets

1 **Family support**—Family life provides high levels of love and support.

2 **Positive family communication**—Young person and her or his parents(s) communicate positively, and young person is willing to seek advice and counsel from parent(s).

3 **Other adult relationships**—Young person receives support from three or more nonparent adults.

4 **Caring neighborhood**—Young person experiences caring neighbors.

5 **Caring school climate**—School provides a caring, encouraging environment.

6 **Parent involvement in schooling**—Parent(s) are actively involved in helping young person succeed in school.

How Young People Experience Support

What's Supportive?

Those who are best at determining what's supportive are those who receive the support, not those who give it, say researchers.

Did You Know?

- During 8th and 9th grade, only 39 percent of students report experiencing asset #3 (other adult relationships).
- Less than half of young people (40 percent) report living in caring neighborhoods.

The Support Assets: How They Stack Up

The six support assets are essential in providing a solid foundation for children and teenagers. Based on Search Institute surveys of almost 100,000 young people in 213 communities, the following percentages of young people report having these assets:

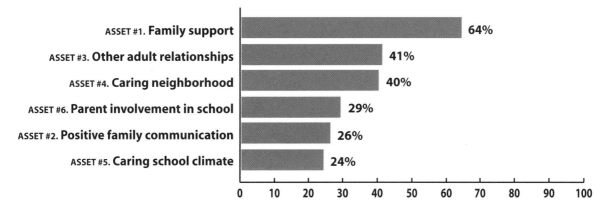

ASSET #1. **Family support**	64%
ASSET #3. **Other adult relationships**	41%
ASSET #4. **Caring neighborhood**	40%
ASSET #6. **Parent involvement in school**	29%
ASSET #2. **Positive family communication**	26%
ASSET #5. **Caring school climate**	24%

0 10 20 30 40 50 60 70 80 90 100

Everyday Asset Building

Lynn Stambaugh, the parent of four children ages 9 to 14 in Denver, Colorado, thought about all the adults who regularly interacted with her kids. She made a list of these adults. It included teachers, coaches, music teachers, janitors, bus drivers, and so on.

In a letter to each adult, she wrote: "As an adult working with young people, you play a very important role in the lives of our youth in these very hard-to-grow-up years." She highlighted which assets she saw the particular adult building, mentioning the research behind the assets. "You make a difference," she concluded. "Thank you for all your hard work."

Many of the adults thanked Stambaugh in return! "The letters build awareness," Stambaugh says. "They help make assets a common language."

Supporting Young People

Here are a few ideas for building the six support assets for children and youth at different ages. We've left spaces for you to jot down other ideas you think of or hear about.

Birth to Age 5

- Smile and make eye contact whenever you see a young child. Call the child by name.
- Say yes to children at least as much as you say no. This doesn't mean giving in when you must stay firm. Just be sure the child hears positive messages, too.
- Cheer children on as they master new skills, and be available to comfort and guide them when they get frustrated.
- Encourage children's thinking abilities by asking them questions and exposing them to new situations.
- Play with children, letting them choose the type of play.

- _____
  _____
- _____
  _____

Ages 6 to 11

- Follow their passions and interests, no matter how different they are from your own. Open yourself up to enjoying an activity as much as the child does.
- Answer children's questions. If you don't know, admit this and find out the answers.
- Attend the games, plays, or recitals of children you baby-sit or know in your neighborhood.

- _____
  _____
- _____
  _____

Ages 12 to 18

- Be available to listen.
- Encourage young people to be both independent *and* able to work with others.
- Find out what the teenagers you know or go to school with care about, and help them advocate for their causes.
- If you're an adult, ask teenagers for their opinion or advice on something important.
- If you're a teenager, help your friends succeed. You could slip a note in their lockers if they have a big test coming up. Or make a special sack lunch for a friend who is extremely busy or stressed.
- Provide a safe place where you live for young people to hang out while you're home.

- _____
  _____
- _____
  _____

Your Greatest Supporters

Each of us can think of people who have been important sources of support for us. Sometimes we forget all the ways they showed their support.

Think of two people who are or have been wonderful supporters for you. Write each person's name in the circle (or draw a picture!). Then think about the things they do or did for or with you. Jot down in the rectangle some specific ways of showing support that are or were particularly important to you.

. . . showed me support by . . .

. . . showed me support by . . .

Reflecting on Your Memories

- What was it about the things these people did that made the support so significant to you?
- How have those experiences shaped the way you show care and support for others?
- What's one thing you could do for or with young people that would honor the way your supporters made a difference in your own life?
- If these people are still living, how can you thank them for the important role they played in your life?

EXPLORING IDEAS

Ways You Can Build Support

No doubt you'll have many ideas of ways to build support as you think about asset building in your life. Here are a few that others have tried and found helpful. We've also left some places for you to write in ideas that come to you.

Where You Live

- Talk with those who live with you about the communication in your household. Is it positive? Does it create an air of openness and trust? How could you improve communication?
- Vow to say at least one encouraging thing to someone in your household every day.
- Stay regularly involved in the lives of the people with whom you live. If you live alone, choose one family member or friend with whom to maintain an ongoing relationship.

- _____
  _____
- _____
  _____

In an Organization

- Learn the names of people in the organization. Take time to talk and offer support for things going on in people's lives outside of work, even if it's for only a few minutes.
- Discuss ways your organization can better support young people in your community. Choose one new thing to do and start it now.

- _____
  _____
- _____
  _____

In Your Neighborhood

- Introduce yourself to one family in your neighborhood whom you have not met. Then find out more about each family member.
- Go out of your way to talk to the children and young people who live near you. Ask questions about their lives and activities.

- _____
  _____
- _____
  _____

Showing Others Your Support

Building the six support assets requires knowing how to support many different kinds of people. Sometimes that may seem easy and obvious, but not always. The truth is that supporting certain people comes more naturally to us than supporting others. Here are some steps to supporting others.

Step 1: Single out someone to support. Choose someone in your extended family, someone in your neighborhood, at your school, or on your team, or someone you come into contact with on a regular basis.

Step 2: Get together with the person. This can be easy and unstructured. For example, if the person is a neighbor, go over and greet her or him when you see each other outside. Make a "date" to get together to do something you both enjoy. You also can do this by phone or by sending a letter or e-mail.

Step 3: Strike up a conversation. Ask how the person is doing. If he or she just says "fine," tell a little bit about yourself, such as "I just heard the best song on the radio." Remember that you don't have to do all the talking. Take the time to listen to what the other person is saying.

Step 4: If you get stumped, say so. Sometimes new relationships can feel uncomfortable. If that happens, say something like, "I really want to get to know you, but I'm not sure what to talk about right now. Got any ideas?"

Step 5: Monitor the other person's reactions. Some people like closeness; others prefer a little distance. Some like to talk about their feelings, while other people are more private. Be respectful of the other person's preferences.

Step 6: Keep in touch. Showing someone your support requires that you keep in contact on a regular basis. Call or sit down to talk regularly, even if just for a few minutes. Continuity is the key, not necessarily the amount of time spent. If it helps, come up with "excuses" to connect—celebrate birthdays, offer to help on a project.

Circles of Your Support

"The neighborhoods that we shape eventually shape our children."
Richard Louv
101 Things You Can Do for Our Children's Future

Children and youth whose lives you touch through decisions you make and through charitable contributions

Children and youth you see but with whom you don't really have a relationship

Children and youth you spend time with occasionally

Children and youth you spend time with regularly

Family members

Little Things Mean a Lot

It isn't necessary to make huge commitments to be able to support children and teenagers. While major personal commitments—such as one-to-one mentoring—can have a tremendous impact, you don't have to start there. Start small. Focus on supporting children and young people in two ways. First, choose one simple thing to show every child or teenager you meet that you care. Then think of one child or youth you will or do support in many ways over a long period of time.

One Simple Action for the Good of All

Review this chapter and choose one easy way you can start supporting many young people now. It may be an idea from these pages. Better yet, come up with ideas that work with the children and young people you know. Then begin with all the young people you meet.

One Simple Action for the Good of One

Choose one young person (a relative, a neighbor, a team-mate, a family friend, a classmate, etc.) to whom you will make a long-term commitment.

Once a month, support her or him in a new way:

- Call on the telephone.
- Send a postcard.
- Contribute to her or his collection.
- Stop by and visit.
- Go out for ice cream.
- Play a game together.
- Do something the child or young person really wants to do.
- Create a celebration.
- Send an e-mail.

CHAPTER 3

A Chance to Contribute

The four empowerment assets are about visions, dreams, and opportunities. When young people feel safe, serve others, and perceive that others value them, they can take healthy risks and try new challenges. Instead of feeling self-conscious and being overwhelmed with worry or fear, they can experiment with new ideas and activities. They discover what they have to offer the world and how their lives can make a positive difference.

That doesn't mean young people won't make mistakes or find times when life is difficult. Everyone messes up sometimes. Everyone is faced with giant obstacles and tricky problems that aren't easily solved. But empowered youth bounce back from mistakes. They know who they can count on when the going gets tough, and they know that difficult times will get better.

The empowerment assets remind us that each young person has her or his own strengths and talents. Young people need to be encouraged to expand their skills and be given meaningful activities that stretch them and bring them a sense of satisfaction and accomplishment. Teenagers from diverse congregations across Boston, for example, found and flexed the power of their collective voice by lobbying the Massachusetts Transportation Authority to extend youth bus/train pass hours so that all students in the area could participate in and get home from after-school activities. Empowered children and teenagers know they can make a difference in the world.

? What Is Empowerment?

Young people need to be valued by their community and have opportunities to contribute to others. For this to occur, they must be safe and feel secure.

The Four Empowerment Assets

7 **Community values youth**—Young person perceives that adults in the community value youth.

8 **Youth as resources**—Young people are given useful roles in the community.

9 **Service to others**—Young person serves in the community one hour or more per week.

10 **Safety**—Young person feels safe at home, at school, and in the neighborhood.

How Young People Experience Empowerment

How Service to Others Helps Young People

Not only do young people who serve others tend to develop caring values, but service also often leads them to think about issues important to themselves and society. Researchers Miranda Yates and James Youniss in the *Journal of Research on Adolescence* found that service projects usually provoke young people to think about:

- Their own lives in comparison to the lives of people who are different from them.
- Their relationship to people who are less fortunate than they are.
- Political and moral questions.
- Their role in bringing about change in society.

Community Perceptions

Two of the empowerment assets deal with community perceptions. They are:
- Asset #7. Community values youth
- Asset #8. Youth as resources

Of the 40 developmental assets, these two are among the assets reported by the fewest youth. How can communities empower young people? How can we help young people be valued and feel it?

The Empowerment Assets: How They Stack Up

The four empowerment assets are a helpful barometer in measuring how valued young people feel. Based on Search Institute surveys of almost 100,000 young people in 213 communities, the following percentages of young people report having these assets:

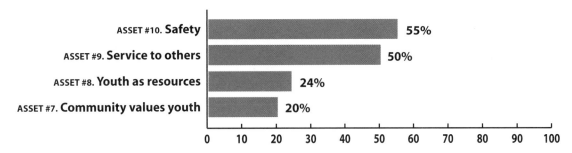

BUILDING ASSETS THROUGH THE YEARS

Empowering Young People

Here are a few ideas for building the four empowerment assets for children and youth at different ages. We've left spaces for you to jot down other ideas you think of or hear about:

Birth to Age 5

- Respond immediately to infants' cries and needs.
- Encourage parents to prop up babies and hold young children so they can see more.
- Childproof all environments where children play to ensure safety.
- Allow and encourage children to try new things on their own, instead of assuming they always need your help.
- Develop the concept of community service by having children do simple tasks at home, such as putting a pot away in a cupboard or putting towels on shelves.
- Do simple acts of community service together, such as collecting food for a food bank.
- Allow children to make simple choices.
- Teach children basic safety rules, such as avoiding poisons.

- _____
  _____
- _____
  _____

Ages 6 to 11

- Encourage children to write letters to the editor or to companies when they have ideas to share or concerns to express.
- Ask children what they like and do not like about their daily routines. Make changes based on some of their ideas.

- Ask children for their help when you're solving a problem or tackling a task.

- _____
  _____
- _____
  _____

Ages 12 to 18

- Invite teenagers to volunteer with you at least one hour a week in community service.
- Discuss young people's feelings and fears about safety. Work together to help young people feel safe.
- Help youth find meaningful, enriching ways to spend their time.
- Encourage young people to take leadership roles in addressing issues that concern them. Help them find constructive ways to resolve an issue, rather than just complaining about a problem.

- _____
  _____
- _____
  _____

Valuable Times

When we were children, there were times when we felt empowered and times we felt powerless. That's not too different from the days now when we feel valued and days when we feel we've been treated unfairly.

Think back to your childhood and/or adolescence and answer the questions below.

Amazing People

In the letters "YES," write the names of people who believed in you when you were young.

Amazing Acts

In the exclamation point, write about one or two things that you did as a child that you still find amazing.

Ways You Can Empower Others

No doubt you'll have many ideas of ways to empower others as you think about asset building in your life. Here are a few that others have tried and found helpful. We've also left some places for you to write in ideas that come to you.

Where You Live

- Make sure where you live is child-friendly, even if you don't have children. Keep it childproof for those occasional child visits and have materials on hand that children can use, such as markers, paper, puzzles, and board games.
- Lead by example. Find ways to regularly serve others in the community. Ask neighbors about service activities if you don't know of any. Find volunteer opportunities you can do with a friend or family member.

- _____
  _____
- _____
  _____

In Your Neighborhood

- Create a neighborhood association that meets on a regular basis. Include people of all ages. Give everyone the opportunity to talk, contribute, and create ways to make the neighborhood a safer, more empowering place to live.
- Give your neighborhood an annual checkup. How do your neighbors feel about safety? Do they know the young people?

Do they treat them respectfully? Do young people feel respected and valued by each other?

- _____
  _____
- _____
  _____

In an Organization

- Identify meaningful ways young people can participate in your organization.
- If young people are customers or employees in your organization, ask for their ideas and their help in making the organization better meet their needs.
- Examine your policies and practices. Are they empowering to everyone involved? How about young people? Older people? Singles? Adults with children? How can your organization value people more?

- _____
  _____
- _____
  _____

Asking Someone to Pitch In

Whether you're an adult working with a group of young people or a teenager leading friends or classmates in a project, building empowerment assets will eventually make your efforts more rewarding. Empowerment assets help young people unleash their gifts and talents to contribute to their families, their schools, and their communities. Here are some steps to follow when asking someone to contribute.

Step 1: Identify what needs to be done. People of all ages are more willing to help out when they know what's expected and the results that are hoped for. Involve children and young people in setting goals up front.

Step 2: Create a variety of tasks. Sometimes a specific task may not appeal to someone. Having a selection of tasks (especially ones with different time commitments) to choose from is more empowering. Be willing to join the youth in the task, or find another person who can help.

Step 3: Help young people succeed. Young people will succeed if they know what's expected and if they're given the proper tools and helpful instructions to do what's expected.

Step 4: Don't underestimate the power of asking. An Independent Sector study found that the number one way young people get involved in volunteering is by having someone ask them. While it's true that some people will say no, when you ask, think about those who will say yes.

Step 5: Focus on building relationships in addition to accomplishing the task at hand. People working together to do something are more likely to stick with it if they get to know each other and feel like important people on the team.

Step 6: Ask for feedback. Helpers often have good ideas on how to make a task more efficient or more creative. Ask those involved for their ideas and their suggestions, and then follow through. Implement some of their ideas immediately.

Step 7: Celebrate. Thank helpers for their contributions. Do something in honor of what has been done and those who have contributed.

Great News

DAILY NEWS

Read All about It!

> **"Don't be afraid to give control over to the youth, take a deep breath, say a short prayer, and get out of the way."**
>
> Rasheed Newsom, 19

So often, the news focuses on all the terrible things people do. The headlines are especially negative when children and teenagers are involved. These types of stories can shape attitudes and the way people act around young people. Building assets, on the other hand, encourages us to focus on what's working.

Have you seen children and youth doing something impressive—leading, serving, or making a difference in some way? Such stories may be local, statewide, national, or international. Jot them down on the newspaper here.

By noticing and calling attention to the ways young people are contributing to society, we empower young people and encourage them to continue making a difference.

Everyday Asset Building

"I am always looking for ways to be involved in the community," says 17-year-old Rachel Loeper of Reading, Pennsylvania. When an adult came to her journalism group at Holy Name High School to talk about asset building, Loeper decided she wanted to get involved.

What impressed her most, however, is that the adults took her seriously. She met "several adults who seemed interested in what I had to say."

Loeper is now 1 of 18 young people involved in the community's Youth Action Team, which is trying to make asset building a community-wide effort. The reason for such a high youth involvement? "We asked," says one of the adults.

Worthwhile Contributions

You have a lot to offer children and youth—even if you don't have much time or money. The most valuable asset you have is you. Think about the things that everyone can offer young people in the list below. Then mark the ones that you can offer young people.

How Everyone Can Empower Youth

Adults can ...

- Listen to young people.
- Notice young people's contributions and gifts.
- Ask young people for their advice.
- Include young people in decisions.
- Give young people meaningful roles.
- Help young people make their dreams come true.
- Find out young people's opinions.
- Celebrate young people's accomplishments.
- Take seriously young people's fears and worries.
- Learn the reasons for young people's feelings.
- See young people as important contributors to your community in the present as well as in the future.
- Learn about music, books, and activities that are important to young people.

Young people can ...

- Listen to each other.
- Notice the contributions of each other.
- Seek advice from wise peers.
- Look for meaningful roles and give them to children, too.
- Listen to each other's dreams and encourage reaching for them.
- Be open to the opinions of others, young and older.
- Celebrate your accomplishments and those of other young people and children.
- Listen to the fears and worries of friends and family members and try to understand them, even if you don't feel the same way.
- Learn the reasons for your feelings and those of your peers.
- Know that you and other young people are important members of your community, with much to contribute now and in the future.
- Share with each other and adults the meaning you find in music, books, and activities.

Imagine your neighborhood or organization as a safe and empowering place for young people. How would adults and young people interact?

How would people feel about living in this kind of neighborhood or being in this kind of organization?

How could you start creating this empowering, safe neighborhood or organization?

CHAPTER 4

Boundaries That Teach

Many people think of discipline when they look at the six boundaries-and-expectations assets. Yet, too often people think of discipline in negative terms and as punishment. The Latin word for discipline means "to teach." Teaching is what these assets are all about—teaching what's admirable and what's not; teaching what's appropriate and what's inappropriate; teaching what's worthwhile and what's not.

These days it can be hard for young people to learn what's in bounds and what's out of bounds. They may get one message about an important issue at home, a different message from the television, another message at school, and still another message in their congregation. How can adults and other young people help them along their way? Here are some places to start:

1. **It helps to talk together about things that are important.** If you're a teenager, let others know what you value because this helps adult boundary setters understand you better and builds trust.
2. **Limits need to be clear.** Young people deserve to know what's expected of them.
3. **Stay in touch.** Independence needs to be balanced with good communication. Adults can show they care by staying interested, involved, and informed. Teenagers can help by trying out new boundaries and being responsible with them before moving on to the next boundary change.
4. **Role models are important.** Young people need adults and peers who set standards and uphold them, act in ways that are respectable, and show them that some things are worth working and waiting for. Whether you're an adult or a teenager, you can be an important role model. You may already be!
5. **Expect the best of each other.** When adults don't expect much of young people, they may not get much. But if adults expect young people to do their best, chances are good that they will. The same goes

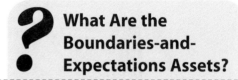

What Are the Boundaries-and-Expectations Assets?

Young people need to know what is expected of them and whether activities and behaviors are "in bounds" or "out of bounds."

The Six Boundaries-and-Expectations Assets

11 **Family boundaries**—Family has clear rules and consequences and monitors the young person's whereabouts.

12 **School boundaries**—School provides clear rules and consequences.

13 **Neighborhood boundaries**—Neighbors take responsibility for monitoring young people's behavior.

14 **Adult role models**—Parent(s) and other adults model positive, responsible behavior.

15 **Positive peer influence**—Young person's best friends model responsible behavior.

16 **High expectations**—Both parent(s) and teachers encourage the young person to do well.

for teenagers' views of adults: Expecting that boundary setting is about who's more powerful will lead to conflict and true power struggles. Expecting that adults will negotiate boundaries in good faith will boost the chances that exactly that will happen.

6. **Accept the best each has to offer.** No one's perfect—no teenager or adult. So temper your expectations to match personalities and experiences.

How Young People Experience Boundaries and Expectations

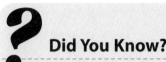 **Did You Know?**

- A higher percentage of girls than boys report having each of the boundaries-and-expectations assets, except for one. The same percentage of boys and girls say they have asset #16 (high expectations).

- All the assets in this category slide between 6th and 12th grade. The asset with the largest drop? Asset #12 (school boundaries). While 70 percent of 6th graders report having this asset, only 34 percent of 12th graders do.

The Boundaries-and-Expectations Assets: How They Stack Up

The six boundaries-and-expectations assets provide young people important information that keeps them safe and lets them stretch and grow. Based on Search Institute surveys of almost 100,000 young people in 213 communities, the following percentages of young people report having these assets:

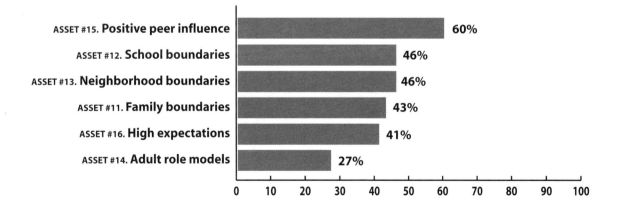

ASSET #15. **Positive peer influence** — 60%
ASSET #12. **School boundaries** — 46%
ASSET #13. **Neighborhood boundaries** — 46%
ASSET #11. **Family boundaries** — 43%
ASSET #16. **High expectations** — 41%
ASSET #14. **Adult role models** — 27%

BUILDING ASSETS THROUGH THE YEARS

Boundaries and Expectations

Here are a few ideas for building the six boundaries-and-expectations assets for children and youth at different ages. We've left spaces for you to jot down other ideas you think of or hear about.

Birth to Age 5

- Realize that babies don't intentionally violate standards and boundaries. Don't punish young children for violating boundaries they can't comprehend.
- Distract children from inappropriate behavior and show them how you want them to act.
- Give simple, understandable boundaries, such as "sit down" or "don't bite."
- Enforce boundaries consistently so children learn them more easily.
- Be calm when children act out in highly emotional ways.
- Learn what to expect from preschoolers. Books and magazines often have useful tips.

- _____
  _____
- _____
  _____

Ages 6 to 11

- Encourage schools, neighbors, organizations, and communities to have consistent boundaries and consequences so children know how to act in different settings.
- Be firm about safety boundaries.

- _____
  _____
- _____
  _____

Ages 12 to 18

Adults:
- Be patient, calm, and consistent as young teenagers test the boundaries you set.
- Negotiate new boundaries as youth grow older. Work together on what's acceptable and what's not. If discussions get heated, have a cooling-off period, and then try again.
- Help teenagers think about future goals and the boundaries required to meet them.
- Respect young people's privacy needs while showing interest in their friends and activities.

- _____
  _____
- _____
  _____

Teenagers:
- Be sure you understand the thinking behind boundaries you've been asked to live with. Help others understand this as well, especially younger adolescents who are struggling to gain more freedoms.
- When you know a boundary needs to change, find a way to explain this calmly but passionately. Set a time to talk. And realize that sometimes change takes more time than you want. Try to be patient.

- _____
  _____
- _____
  _____

Boundaries That Teach

What Was In? What Was Out?

How were you expected to behave when you were a child? Did you have boundaries and expectations? List any boundaries and expectations you were given when you were younger. For example, a behavior that was in might have been: respecting your elders. A behavior that was out might have been: whining for what you wanted.

How did those boundaries and expectations help you? frustrate you? hurt you?

How would you establish boundaries and expectations that are different from when you grew up? What would you keep?

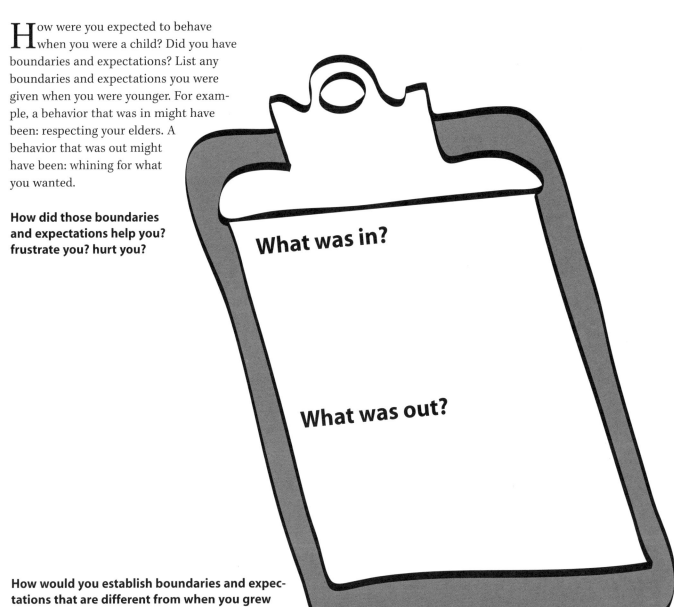

What was in?

What was out?

EXPLORING IDEAS

Ways to Expect the Best

No doubt you'll have many ideas of ways to expect the best as you think about asset building in your life. Here are a few that others have tried and found helpful. We've also left some places for you to write in ideas that come to you.

Where You Live

- Follow the four Cs of boundaries and expectations. Be *clear* about what you expect of youth (if you're an adult) and what's expected of you (if you're a teen). Be *concise;* the shorter the explanation the better. Be *creative;* cleverly stated boundaries and expectations may be easier to "swallow." Be *consistent* in upholding (or observing) them.
- Hang up a calendar or wipe-off board so everyone in the family can mark when they're going somewhere, who they're with, and when they'll be back.

- _____
  _____
- _____
  _____

In Your Neighborhood

- Before setting neighborhood boundaries, work first on creating a caring neighborhood to build trust and respect among young adults and young people. Have a neighborhood block party, cookie exchange, barbecue, or pizza party.
- Get together with other neighbors and discuss boundaries. Find three that everyone agrees on to enforce informally in the neighborhood.

- _____
  _____
- _____
  _____

In an Organization

- If your organization sponsors youth activities, establish clear ground rules and consequences for youth participation. Address how youth are expected to treat each other, adult leaders, and property. Involve youth in setting expectations for how adults treat and respect them.
- Identify ways your organization can enrich, challenge, and stretch young people. What opportunities can you provide so that young people gain new insights and learn new skills? In what ways can your organization benefit from involving youth?

- _____
  _____
- _____
  _____

Setting Boundaries and Expectations

Expectations and boundaries are like the solid and dotted yellow lines on the road. These lines aren't good or bad—they simply give us helpful information. Everyone needs to know behavioral lane markers as they journey through childhood and adolescence. Here are some steps in setting boundaries and expectations:

Step 1: Examine your attitudes about boundaries and expectations. Typically our childhood experiences dictate our views on the subject. People may do the opposite of what they grew up with. Adults who had many strict boundaries as children can be reluctant to set boundaries. Those who had few boundaries may err in setting too many. When you're in a position to set boundaries and expectations, it helps to reflect first on how your background colors your viewpoint.

Step 2: Brainstorm ideas on boundaries. It's often tempting for adults to start creating a list of boundaries as young people begin to act in ways that they don't like. Instead, it's better to be proactive and come up with a simple, solid list of boundaries. The best ideas come out when adults, teenagers, and children are involved in brainstorming together. In fact, young people may even come up with more stringent boundaries than adults.

Step 3: Discuss the values that are the basis for boundaries and expectations. People who value a lifelong commitment to learning often have high expectations about homework and attending school. Those who value honesty will stress the importance of telling the truth when accidents and misbehavior happen. Values typically form the foundation for helpful boundaries and expectations.

Step 4: Create a sense of win-win on boundaries and expectations. Work together on the list and come up with expectations that everyone agrees on.

Step 5: Keep the final list simple and short. Some neighborhoods make the list simple: "Neighbors are to respect each other and each other's property." That one boundary actually says a lot.

Step 6: Post the boundaries. Put boundaries and expectations in writing and distribute them. Post them at the neighborhood park, laundromat, community center, or any other place neighbors congregate. This gives the list of boundaries and expectations more exposure.

Step 7: Be consistent in reinforcing boundaries and expectations. Guidelines mean nothing if no one notices or says anything about whether the guidelines are met or not.

The State of Boundaries Today

Think about young people today. Overall, do you feel young people in your neighborhood have the boundaries-and-expectations assets?

Looking at each of the six boundaries-and-expectations assets, rate how you think these assets are being instilled in young people today, with 1 being "standards are too low," 3 being "standards are just right," and 5 being "standards are too high."

> *"Rather than telling children what to do, tell a story with a lesson so they can decide for themselves."*
>
> From *Helping Kids Succeed— Alaska Style*

Asset #11.	Family boundaries	1	2	3	4	5
Asset #12.	School boundaries	1	2	3	4	5
Asset #13.	Neighborhood boundaries	1	2	3	4	5
Asset #14.	Adult role models	1	2	3	4	5
Asset #15.	Positive peer influence	1	2	3	4	5
Asset #16.	High expectations	1	2	3	4	5

What do you think needs to happen so that these assets are being built for and with young people today? How can you contribute to this boundary building?

Everyday Asset Building

On a hot summer day, three young teenagers rode their bikes through an alley, swearing louder than a boom box cranked to the loudest volume. Jeff Roy, president of the Lennox Neighborhood Association in St. Louis Park, Minnesota, immediately shouted, "Hey!" to get their attention and then said firmly and calmly, "In this neighborhood we don't talk that way."

Within 10 seconds, Roy had made it clear what the expectations for behavior were. But setting boundaries and enforcing them is easier if you know the young people first, Roy notes. "Use every opportunity you can to let children know you like them," he advocates. "It's a risk sometimes, and it takes energy. But there's no shortcut to building a society."

The Importance of Fences— *Short* Ones

Many people feel uncomfortable with asset #13 (neighborhood boundaries). It's easy to think of neighborhood boundaries like those tall privacy fences. The attitude today often is, Keep your nose out of my business, and I'll keep my nose out of yours.

Asset building isn't about building tall fences between each other. It's more like setting up some short picket fences that let us know where it's appropriate to walk and where it isn't—fences that give our lives some boundaries. These fences aren't isolating or intimidating. They clearly mark the boundaries, and they are attractive.

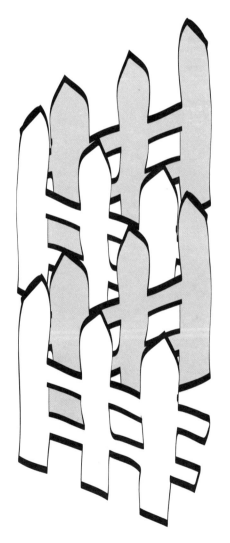

What boundaries and expectations would you like your family, school, neighborhood, or organization to have?

What's your role in establishing and monitoring boundaries in your family, school, neighborhood, or organization?

What would help you feel more comfortable in building boundaries in your family, school, neighborhood, or organization?

CHAPTER 5

Time Well Spent

The four constructive-use-of-time assets show that *how* children and teenagers spend their time makes a big difference in the way they grow up. What do these assets offer young people?

- **Balance.** The constructive-use-of-time assets encourage young people to get involved in creative activities, youth programs, and congregational programs. They also say young people need to spend time at home with their families.
- **Connections.** Through activities, young people have opportunities to build relationships with caring peers and caring adults.
- **Challenges.** Most constructive activities challenge young people to grow and learn. These challenges help children and young people expand their horizons and try new things.
- **Safe places.** For many young people, youth programs provide a safe, supervised place to spend time. Without them, young people may spend many hours alone, which too often can lead to dangerous or negative activities.
- **Growth.** Constructive activities give young people opportunities to grow.

When young people spend their time in meaningful ways, everyone benefits. Young people learn new skills and connect to a great variety of people. Adults share their passions along with their skills. Neighborhoods and communities benefit from energized, excited young people who feel empowered and are willing to contribute their talents and their ideas.

? What Are the Constructive-Use-of-Time Assets?

Young people need constructive, enriching opportunities for growth through creative activities, youth programs, congregational involvement, and quality time at home.

The Four Constructive-Use-of-Time Assets

17 **Creative activities**—Young person spends three or more hours per week in lessons or practice in music, theater, or other arts.

18 **Youth programs**—Young person spends three or more hours per week in sports, clubs, or organizations at school and/or in the community.

19 **Religious community**—Young person spends one or more hours per week in activities in a religious institution.

20 **Time at home**—Young person is out with friends "with nothing special to do" two or fewer nights per week.

Making the Most of Time

The Power of Faith Community

Although talking about faith is a sensitive issue, especially in public schools, young people who are involved in a faith community are more likely to grow up healthy than youth who aren't involved. Search Institute researchers compared young people who were active in faith communities with young people who weren't active and found some big differences. Those who were involved were much less likely to have sexual intercourse, binge drink, ride with a driver who had been drinking, smoke, and use illicit drugs.

The Constructive-Use-of-Time Assets: How They Stack Up

These four assets show how young people spend their time and how they don't spend their time. Based on Search Institute surveys of almost 100,000 young people in 213 communities, the following percentages of young people report having these assets:

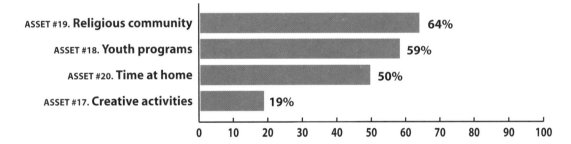

Everyday Asset Building

When her town of Robbinsdale, Minnesota, began creating an asset-building community, Linda Kemper realized that her role as a person involved with young people wasn't over. "I have a responsibility as a resident in the community. I can be there for kids," she says.

Even though Kemper has a son who is grown, she decided she could still contribute to the other young people in her neighborhood. So she put up a basket-ball hoop and invited the neighborhood youth to use it. Two children who live nearby, Kirstin and Teddy, play basketball at Kemper's hoop a lot. They say that Kemper keeps an eye on them, administers first aid when they get hurt, supports their improving basketball skills, and cheers them on.

"I can build assets in kids, even though they're not my kids," Kemper says. Then she pauses briefly before adding, "But they *are* my kids." ✍

BUILDING ASSETS THROUGH THE YEARS

Making Time Meaningful for Young People

Here are a few ideas for building the four constructive-use-of-time assets for children and youth at different ages. We've left spaces for you to jot down other ideas you think of or hear about.

Birth to Age 5

- Be flexible with an infant's schedule and gradually introduce predictable routines.
- Have babies and toddlers spend most of their time with their parent(s) or consistent caregivers.
- Balance stimulating, structured time with free playtime.
- Have consistent times for children to sleep, eat, play, and relax.
- Introduce preschoolers to museums, theater, and events that welcome children.

- _____
  _____
- _____
  _____

Ages 6 to 11

- Allow children to have one or two out-of-home activities that are led by caring adults.
- Teach children the skill of balancing their time so they gradually learn to keep busy but not too busy.

- _____
  _____
- _____
  _____

Age 12 to 18

- Families: Have a regular night to do something fun together.
- Adults: Help young people look for positive, stimulating activities that match their talents, interests, and abilities. Help with rides or other arrangements if needed.
- Teenagers: Get involved in at least one activity that may continue into your adult years.
- Parents: Help young people think about how time spent on different activities helps or hinders in reaching their goals. Evaluate how much "hanging out" time your teenager has.

- _____
  _____
- _____
  _____

Meaningful Memories

Think back to when you were younger. What were some of the meaningful ways you spent time? Which do you still cherish? List them on the easel. Think about all four of the assets: #17 (creative activities), #18 (youth programs), #19 (religious community), and #20 (time at home). Star the memory that was your favorite. What activities could youth today do that would give them similar experiences?

My Favorite Activities

Exploring Ideas

Ways to Make Time Meaningful

No doubt you'll have many ideas of ways to make time meaningful as you think about asset building in your life. Here are a few that others have tried and found helpful. We've also left some places for you to write in ideas that come to you.

Where You Live

- Turn off your television.
- Spend meaningful, enjoyable time together as a family on a regular basis. Find activities that give you something to *do* together but that also open up opportunities to talk to each other and share your dreams and hopes.
- Keep a balance between outside activities and spending time at home, with young people able to participate in a limited number of activities at school, in the community, and/or in a congregation. But be sure there's also plenty of family time.

- _____
  _____
- _____
  _____

In Your Neighborhood

- Identify nearby activities for young people. Consider organizing shared transportation so that many neighborhood youth can participate easily.
- If there's a park in the neighborhood, get together to organize regular activities that young people can count on.

- Find out what neighbors like to do. Create a neighborhood softball or basketball team, and challenge a block nearby to a game. Organize a talent show. Or have a neighborhood craft and hobby day.

- _____
  _____
- _____
  _____

In an Organization

- Survey your community to see how many youth program opportunities exist for young people. Promote what's available. If young people aren't using what's available, find out why and try to remove or reduce obstacles.
- Volunteer to help lead some type of youth activity. Find an opportunity that fits your own talents and interests.

- _____
  _____
- _____
  _____

BUILDING SKILLS

Making the Best Use of Your Time

The four constructive-use-of-time assets focus on time well spent. They give us a clear picture of how to become well-rounded people. Whether you're an adult or youth, these are some steps that can help you make the best use of your time.

Step 1: Figure out what captures your interest. It's tempting to throw out a particular constructive-use-of-time asset, citing that we don't have any talent or interest in it. All of us can find a creative activity that interests us. The same is true of faith communities. Finding the faith community that is a good "fit" may be a challenge, but there is likely one out there that's for you.

Step 2: Keep trying. It may take a while to find the activities that you enjoy, but if you focus on finding *something*, you'll get there a lot faster.

Step 3: Watch your mix of activities. Making the most of our time is finding a balance between the four assets in this category.

Step 4: Rethink your ideas on time management. Many people think that managing time well means getting more done in less time. Just remember that pursuing a passion often involves investing a lot of time and energy in something you love—and that's good, too!

Step 5: Get to know others around you. The benefits of activities are not only learning new skills but also getting to know some really great people. Be deliberate about building relationships along the way.

Step 6: Evaluate activities along the way. Activities change as they go along—and so can your interest in them. Be honest about your feelings and be willing to make changes if you lose interest or find something different that captures your imagination.

LOOKING AROUND

Where Have You Been?

Imagine that children and youth put labels on their bookbags to show where they've been. On the bookbag, list all the places children and youth spend their time in your community. Where are they welcome? Where are they safe? Where is their positive adult supervision?

> "An asset-building community works to protect time for families to be together."
>
> Peter Benson
> President, Search Institute

It's Time to Make a Difference

Think about how you spend your time. Look at your schedule for the next month. Where can you find some time to build assets for and with young people? How can you incorporate it into what you already do? Start small. It's okay if you have only a few minutes at first or if you have an hour.

How much time can you spend?

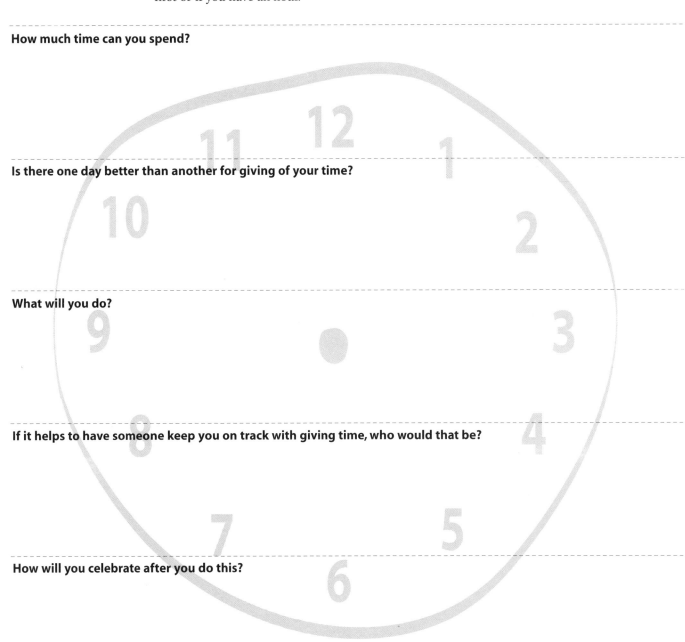

Is there one day better than another for giving of your time?

What will you do?

If it helps to have someone keep you on track with giving time, who would that be?

How will you celebrate after you do this?

CHAPTER 6

Learning for a Lifetime

A commitment to learning is a commitment to growing. When we learn something new, we grow, change, and expand our horizons. This is true whether one is age 2, 14, or 60. The commitment-to-learning assets are built for children and youth through adults' attitudes, encouragement, involvement, and modeling. Young people look to their teachers, parents, and neighbors to learn new information, ideas, and perspectives.

There's a lot of concern about young people's education and their commitment to learning. Fortunately, there are practical ways everyone can encourage learning:

- **Model curiosity and discovery.** A commitment to learning is contagious. Adults can inspire young people to learn, focusing on why education is important, how it has shaped their lives, and how it can be fun, stimulating, and rewarding. Young people can inspire adults and children to explore new topics, ideas, and issues.
- **Read with young people and encourage them to read on their own.** Whether it's reading aloud to younger children, giving books to older youth, or reading and discussing novels with fellow high school students, find ways to encourage reading.
- **Make learning relevant.** Young people benefit from seeing how learning applies to working and to life. If you have a job, volunteer in a school to talk about how your work or career has ties to schoolwork.
- **Be an advocate for effective schools.** If you're 18 or older, be sure to vote on school referenda. Speak up in support of good schools when needed. Challenge schools to be strong institutions. Encourage learning for all students, young or older.
- **Highlight learning beyond the classroom.** Learning happens in many different places—in homes, nature, community centers, congregations, workplaces, and parks. Help young people discover the joy of learning in all that they do by asking questions, helping them dig for information, and sharing in their excitement about new information.

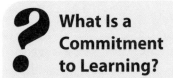

What Is a Commitment to Learning?

Young people need to develop a lifelong commitment to both formal and informal education.

The Five Commitment-to-Learning Assets

21 **Achievement motivation**—Young person is motivated to do well in school.

22 **School engagement**—Young person is actively engaged in learning.

23 **Homework**—Young person reports doing at least one hour of homework every school day.

24 **Bonding to school**—Young person cares about her or his school.

25 **Reading for pleasure**—Young person reads for pleasure three or more hours per week.

How Young People Experience Commitment-to-Learning Assets

 Did You Know?

- Girls are more likely than boys to report having all of the commitment-to-learning assets.

- Eighth graders report having the lowest percentage of three commitment-to-learning assets: asset #21 (achievement motivation), asset #22 (school engagement), and asset #24 (bonding to school).

The Commitment-to-Learning Assets: How They Stack Up

The five commitment-to-learning assets show how much young people are motivated to learn. Based on Search Institute surveys of almost 100,000 young people in 213 communities, the following percentages of young people report having these assets:

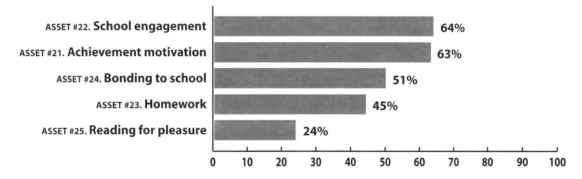

ASSET #22. **School engagement** — 64%
ASSET #21. **Achievement motivation** — 63%
ASSET #24. **Bonding to school** — 51%
ASSET #23. **Homework** — 45%
ASSET #25. **Reading for pleasure** — 24%

0 10 20 30 40 50 60 70 80 90 100

Everyday Asset Building

Carrie and Tom Barndt believe that all young people need time to study. Since they own four McDonald's restaurants in Madison, Wisconsin, they created the McStudy program for their student employees. Through McStudy, young people can add one hour of paid study time before or after their work shifts, up to three hours a week. They also give student employees generous leaves of absence when they need time for sport activities or rehearsals.

"This helps us keep good people," says Carrie Barndt. "Before the program, students who valued learning would work only for the summer and then quit for the school year. Now, they can keep working year round—and still value their commitment to learning."

Helping Young People Learn

Here are a few ideas for building the five commitment-to-learning assets for children and youth at different ages. We've left spaces for you to jot down other ideas you think of or hear about.

Birth to Age 5

- Give safe, interesting things to babies and toddlers to look at and touch, such as household objects or toys in different colors, shapes, and sizes.
- Sing and read to babies, toddlers, and preschoolers daily.
- Expose toddlers and preschoolers to new environments, such as parks and stores.
- Make a game for children to learn names of objects.
- Talk about what you see and hear whenever you are with a child and ask the child to talk about what he or she sees and hears.

- _____
  _____
- _____
  _____

Ages 6 to 11

- Set up a place to do homework, and set daily homework guidelines.
- Let children read to you every day as they learn to read. Celebrate their first reading!

- _____
  _____
- _____
  _____

Ages 12 to 18

- Find creative ways to link personal interests with school subjects. Discover the historical roots of rock, hip-hop, or jazz music for a history project.
- Contribute to collections that strengthen learning.
- Adults: Help teenagers think about their goals and the education and discipline required to reach them.
- Place more emphasis on lifelong learning rather than focusing only on graduation.
- Do things that use different parts of the brain and ways of learning. Comment on progress when you see someone (adult or youth) gaining new insights or being able to think in new ways.

- _____
  _____
- _____
  _____

Your History of Learning

Think about what you have really enjoyed learning. Name two areas of learning that you remember when you were younger and two areas of learning that took place recently. Write one area of learning next to each pencil. Then briefly explain what got you interested in that topic. (Remember that learning takes place everywhere—at school, at work, at home, in nature, in the neighborhood.) How could this experience translate in today's time?

EXPLORING IDEAS

Ways You Can Emphasize Learning

No doubt you'll have many ideas of ways to emphasize learning as you think about asset building in your life. Here are a few that others have tried and found helpful. We've also left some places for you to write in ideas that come to you.

Where You Live

- Make where you live a center of learning. Keep it stocked with as many books, art supplies, and magazines as you can. Some thrift stores offer these items at very low cost.
- Talk daily about something new: current events, a topic everyone is interested in, or a family project (such as building a table together).
- Set reading goals. Try to read one book per month.

- _____
  _____
- _____
  _____

In an Organization

- Encourage employees to volunteer to read books aloud at nearby schools.
- Offer work career shadowing, internships, and limited part-time jobs (no more than 15 hours per week during the school year) for students to expose them to career opportunities.
- Youth: Tell adults about books or articles in magazines that will help them learn about topics that interest you. Later, have a conversation about the topic.

- _____
  _____
- _____
  _____

In Your Neighborhood

- Ask neighbors to include their areas of expertise (computers, math, English, arts) in a "homework helpers" list to distribute to students. Then encourage students to call neighbors when they need specific help.
- Have an annual neighborhood book swap. Ask neighbors to donate books they've already read, and have everyone come to find new books.

- _____
  _____
- _____
  _____

Becoming a Lifelong Learner

Becoming a lifelong learner involves opening our minds and our hearts.

Step 1: Recognize the learning that is happening all around you. While it's true that a lot of learning happens in a classroom, it also happens everywhere. Look around for new information to soak up, new skills to acquire, and new practices to try.

Step 2: Value learning for its own sake. Too often we use rewards and incentives to motivate ourselves and others to accomplish an educational task. Researcher and author Teresa Amabile found that children were more creative when they weren't promised any rewards for creating a collage. When we tap into the inner motivation in each person, some of the best learning can take place.

Step 3: Be open to a variety of learning experiences. We often have preconceived ideas about what we consider to be "productive" learning versus things that are a "waste of time." Creative learning can often involve a lot of staring off into space, doodling, and what many others see as "goofing around."

Step 4: Be conscious of what you resist learning and what you find easy. Learning involves having a balance between a sense of accomplishment and a sense of challenge. Taking on too much challenge can cause anxiety and make you want to give up. Too much accomplishment can make the process boring after a while.

Step 5: Follow your passions. "Follow your bliss," said author Joseph Campbell, "and doors will open where you didn't know they were going to be." Becoming a lifelong learner means that you're always on a journey to learn more and can't wait to see what your "next destination" will be.

What's Working?

Although each of the assets needs attention, it's sometimes easier to focus on what's not working instead of what is. As you think about the state of learning for young people today, write one example of how you have observed assets being built for each of the commitment-to-learning assets below.

> "A commitment to and interest in lifelong learning may be more important for young people than their mastery of particular information."
>
> Donald Draayer
> National Superintendent of Schools, '90–'91

List as many people as you can think of who help build these assets.

What are their characteristics? Where are you on the list?

What Can You Do?

When it comes to building the commitment-to-learning assets, we each have a lot to give. Some people choose one of the assets and focus their efforts on building it. Others attempt to build all five assets—even in small ways. What about you? How can you help build the commitment-to-learning assets with and for young people?

Write your ideas and challenges on this notebook page. Remember, your ideas do not need to be difficult, expensive, or time-consuming.

CHAPTER 7

Passing Along Positive Values

One dictionary defines a value as "a principle, standard, or quality considered worthwhile or desirable." The word is related to the French word *valoir* (to be worth) and the Latin *valere* (to be strong).

You hear a lot of debate these days about values, but it's clear that our society needs to nurture worthwhile principles, standards, and qualities in children and young people to help make them strong. Values become an inner compass that young people can use to guide them in making choices in a confusing world. Indeed, a 1997 *US News and World Report* poll of 1,000 adults found that teaching children values and discipline was considered the most important issue facing education today. It is also the job of each of us, not just schools.

While we may never agree on *all* the values that are important for young people, most people can agree on a few. The six positive-values assets are one way of naming a set of positive principles, standards, and qualities that virtually everyone can affirm. In many senses, positive values do give the strength that's suggested in the Latin word *valere*. When young people feel pulled or pressured to engage in high-risk behavior, the value of restraint gives them strength to resist the temptation. The positive-values assets provide the foundation for young people's character. Sure, there are many other values that may be equally important for young people. But we can get started by building these six values for all children and youth.

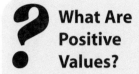

What Are Positive Values?

Young people need to develop strong values that shape their character and guide their choices.

The Six Positive-Values Assets

26 **Caring**—Young person places high value on helping other people.

27 **Equality and social justice**—Young person places high value on promoting equality and reducing hunger and poverty.

28 **Integrity**—Young person acts on convictions and stands up for her or his beliefs.

29 **Honesty**—Young person "tells the truth even when it is not easy."

30 **Responsibility**—Young person accepts and takes personal responsibility.

31 **Restraint**—Young person believes it is important not to be sexually active or to use alcohol or other drugs.

FAST FACTS

How Young People Experience the Positive-Values Assets

Keys to Nurturing Values

Researchers have found that children are more likely to develop positive values when their parents:

1. Model positive values;
2. Are not callous or do not reject the child; and
3. Ask the child to be kind and responsible.

Researchers have also found that children and teenagers are more likely to develop positive values if parents support children, asking questions and seeking opinions rather than lecturing or challenging.

One final thing that shows up in research: Young people are more likely to exhibit positive values if people ask them to. That's something everyone—not just parents—can do for young people.

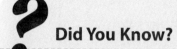

Did You Know?

- Only 32 percent of boys have asset #26 (caring) compared to 54 percent of girls.

- Of the positive-values assets, youth surveyed most commonly reported having asset #28 (integrity), asset #29 (honesty), and asset #30 (responsibility).

The Positive-Values Assets: How They Stack Up

The six positive-values assets are at the core of what develops character in young people. Based on Search Institute surveys of almost 100,000 young people in 213 communities, the following percentages of young people report having these assets:

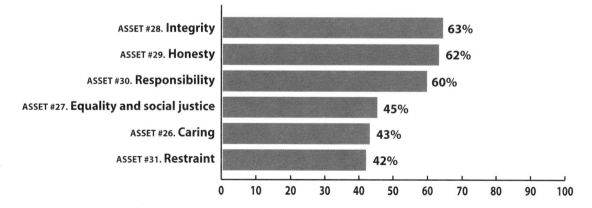

ASSET #28. **Integrity** — 63%
ASSET #29. **Honesty** — 62%
ASSET #30. **Responsibility** — 60%
ASSET #27. **Equality and social justice** — 45%
ASSET #26. **Caring** — 43%
ASSET #31. **Restraint** — 42%

BUILDING ASSETS THROUGH THE YEARS

Promoting Positive Values

Here are a few ideas for building the positive-values assets for children and youth at different ages. We've left spaces for you to jot down other ideas you think of or hear about.

Birth to Age 5

- Create caring atmospheres where you live and at child care centers and other places for young children.
- Articulate your values while modeling and teaching them as children grow.
- Find simple ways for children to care for others, such as by giving hugs and doing nice things to make someone else happy.
- Interact with children in loving, respectful, and caring ways.
- Teach preschoolers how to care for a special toy, outfit, or plant by themselves.
- Explain your values simply to children when you see others behaving in ways that you value or do not value.

- _____
  _____
- _____
  _____

Ages 6 to 11

- Have children write thank-you notes or show their appreciation in some other way whenever they receive gifts.
- Encourage families to participate in service activities together.
- Model restraint and talk about why it's worth it to you to wait for something a little while when the payoff is big later on.

- Tell children about a time when it was hard to tell the truth but you did and felt good about doing so.

- _____
  _____
- _____
  _____

Ages 12 to 18

- Interact in caring, responsible ways with all people—young children, senior citizens, adults, and teenagers.
- Watch a television show, see a movie, or read books together, and discuss the values presented.
- Encourage teenagers to volunteer with at least one organization.
- Together write letters to legislators advocating for or against pending legislation.

- _____
  _____
- _____
  _____

Values Instilled in You

Families often emphasize certain positive values over others. Think about the values your family felt were important when you were a child. Respond to the statements below, thinking about the values your family held. If you're younger than 18, think back as far as you can.

Which values did your family emphasize when you were growing up?

How did those values shape your family?

Think of a story that shows those values at work in your family.

Why do you think your family had the values it did?

How have those values influenced you today?

Ways to Build Positive Values

No doubt you'll have many ideas of ways to build positive values as you think about asset building in your life. Here are a few that others have tried and found helpful. We've also left some places for you to write in ideas that come to you.

Where You Live

- Your actions reveal your true values. Think about what other family members learn about values from the way you talk and act.
- Discuss equality and social justice issues on a regular basis. Choose a cause to follow and support the work of those who are making progress in your area of concern.

- _____
  _____
- _____
  _____

In an Organization

- Develop easy ways for people of all ages in your organization to be able to contribute to worthy causes through their time, their talent, or their money.
- Examine the values that your organization says it stands for. How do employees and volunteers view your organization? How do people in your community view it? How can you model positive values in your organization?

- _____
  _____
- _____
  _____

In Your Neighborhood

- Talk to people of all ages (young or older) in respectful ways.
- When you see a child or youth doing something you disagree with, teach the young person the difference between right and wrong. Help the young person listen to her or his conscience.
- Be sure to ask neighborhood youth to be caring, honest, and responsible. Remind them that these values are important.

- _____
  _____
- _____
  _____

Talking about What's Important to You

Naming the values we cherish is an important part of building these assets. The next step is being able to express our values in ways that build community instead of dividing it. Here are some steps to talking about values.

Step 1: Think through values. Thinking through ideas and talking about our values with people who are closest to us is a good place to start. Being clear about values makes it easier to talk about them with others we don't know as well.

Step 2: Identify emotional hot spots. Some people become upset when talking about values. Sometimes this has to do with personality, but often it has more to do with the experiences a person has had. An extreme emotional reaction rarely helps when talking about our values; however, strong emotional reactions can tell us about our feelings. If we work through these feelings, we can learn what they have to teach about our values and ways each of us can share them appropriately.

Step 3: Look for opportunities to talk about values. Daily conversations present chances to express our values. For example, if someone begins talking about how a neighbor lost his job, we can say, "I'd like to take him a pan of brownies because I want him to know that we care."

Step 4: Be open to other people's insights. Our values are always under construction. We may think they're set and finished, but then somebody says something that makes us think about what we value. This doesn't mean, for example, that if we value responsibility we abandon that value. It means we might get a new insight, like labeling something spontaneous instead of irresponsible.

Step 5: Remember the ultimate value. No value is more important than a person. Values are not about drawing lines in the sand; values are about knowing who we are so that we can build bridges to other people. Even when we're with people who have different values, we can still treat people with dignity and respect without giving up or backing down on our own values. When we value *people* over our opinions, we can enjoy the relationships that develop and grow. In the process of talking with others, we gain more clarity about values, and we will see new ways to live out what we value.

Which Values Are Valued?

Think about your school, neighborhood, club, or congregation today. How much agreement do you think there would be on the six values that are included in the category of positive-values assets? For each asset, check whether almost everyone, most people, some people, or not many people would agree that this asset is important.

	Almost everyone	Most people	Some people	Not many people
ASSET #26. **Caring**	☐	☐	☐	☐
ASSET #27. **Equality and social justice**	☐	☐	☐	☐
ASSET #28. **Integrity**	☐	☐	☐	☐
ASSET #29. **Honesty**	☐	☐	☐	☐
ASSET #30. **Responsibility**	☐	☐	☐	☐
ASSET #31. **Restraint**	☐	☐	☐	☐
TOTAL checkmarks:	____	____	____	____

If most people agree to these assets, what can you do to promote these assets within your community?

> *"So much of life, in today's world, has to do with getting. Values, in contrast, have to do with being and with giving."*
>
> Linda and Richard Eyre
> authors of *Teaching Your Children Values*

What other positive values do you think almost everyone in the community would believe are important for young people? How can you also promote those values?

Everyday Asset Building

In Marquette, Michigan, fifth-grade teacher Jill Koske has cooked up a meaningful way to teach her students about several positive-values assets. Twice a month, the students bake bread and deliver it to residents of Jantzen House, a local transition residence for homeless members of the community and others needing help. Working in teams of four, the students learn cooperation, apply math skills, and discover some basic principles of science. But delivering the bread is the highlight. "We've been to Jantzen House when residents have been there and the children have been humbled by the experience," says Koske.

LOOKING FORWARD

Walk the Talk, Talk the Walk

One of the most important ways to teach positive values is to model them in your own life—to walk your talk. It's also important to talk to others about the values that are behind your actions—to talk your walk.

Think about the six positive-values assets:

- Which value is the easiest for you to live out? What can you do to pass this value along to others in your family, neighborhood, school, organization, or community?
- Which is the most challenging to you? What can you do to make sure that you're modeling this value as much as possible for people in your life?
- In the circles below, jot down what you can do and say in the next two weeks to both "walk your talk" and "talk your walk" for each of the six positive-values assets.

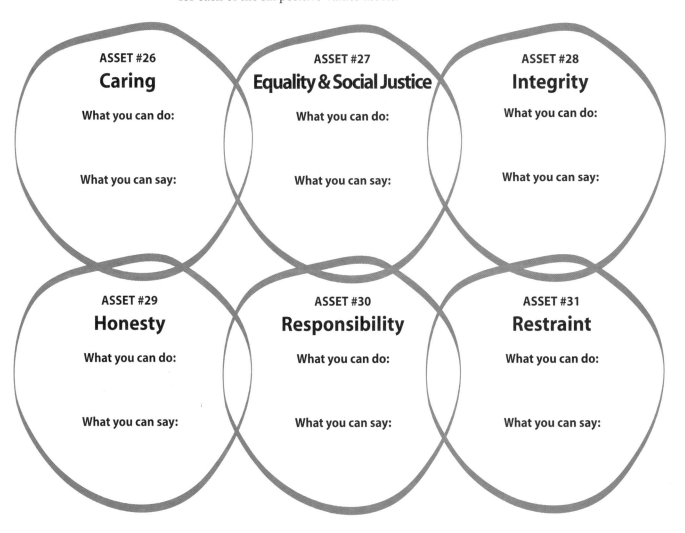

ASSET #26
Caring

What you can do:

What you can say:

ASSET #27
Equality & Social Justice

What you can do:

What you can say:

ASSET #28
Integrity

What you can do:

What you can say:

ASSET #29
Honesty

What you can do:

What you can say:

ASSET #30
Responsibility

What you can do:

What you can say:

ASSET #31
Restraint

What you can do:

What you can say:

CHAPTER 8

Skills for Growing and Living

Social competencies are the skills all people need to navigate successfully through life. Without social competencies, people lack the essential skills they need to live their values, contribute in meaningful ways, get along with others, and be responsible members of society.

How can people learn how to manage money if they don't have planning and decision-making skills? How can people become worthwhile team players on the job if they don't have interpersonal competence and resistance skills? How can we live in a world that is rich in diversity without skills of cultural competence and peaceful conflict resolution?

Learning social competencies is like learning how to play the piano. Rarely does the piano playing sound very good at first. Likewise, to develop basic skills needed for life we need "piano teachers" more than "music critics." We need suggestions for new methods to try and encouragement to keep going when we make mistakes. We need to be cheered on as we learn to master skills.

Young people especially need adults and peers who demonstrate, teach, and practice skills with them. They need adults and peers who watch how they are doing with their skills and who give them feedback along the way. They need people who not only teach them and show them the way, but also let them make and learn from mistakes.

? What Are Social Competencies?

Young people need competencies and skills that equip them to make positive choices, to build relationships, and to succeed in life.

The Five Social-Competencies Assets

32 **Planning and decision making**—Young person knows how to plan ahead and make choices.

33 **Interpersonal competence**—Young person has empathy, sensitivity, and friendship skills.

34 **Cultural competence**—Young person has knowledge of and comfort with people of different cultural/racial/ethnic backgrounds.

35 **Resistance skills**—Young person can resist negative peer pressure and dangerous situations.

36 **Peaceful conflict resolution**—Young person seeks to resolve conflict nonviolently.

How Young People Experience the Social-Competencies Assets

Essential Ingredients of Social Competence

Researcher J. David Hawkins has identified essential skills young people need to develop social competence. They are:

- Identifying, labeling, and expressing feelings.
- Assessing the intensity of feelings and managing them.
- Delaying gratification and controlling impulses.
- Reducing stress.
- Knowing the difference between feelings and actions.
- Being able to read and interpret social cues.
- Using problem-solving and decision-making skills.
- Having positive self-talk.
- Understanding others' perspectives.

Did You Know?

- A higher percentage of girls than boys reports having all the social-competencies assets.
- The biggest gap occurs with asset #33 (interpersonal competence): More than half of girls surveyed (60 percent) report having it, compared with only 26 percent of boys.

- Understanding what behaviors are acceptable and unacceptable.
- Having a positive attitude towards life.
- Developing realistic expectations about themselves.
- Being able to communicate nonverbally and verbally.

The Social-Competencies Assets: How They Stack Up

The five social-competencies assets indicate a number of skills young people need to succeed. Based on Search Institute surveys of almost 100,000 young people in 213 communities, the following percentages of young people report having these assets:

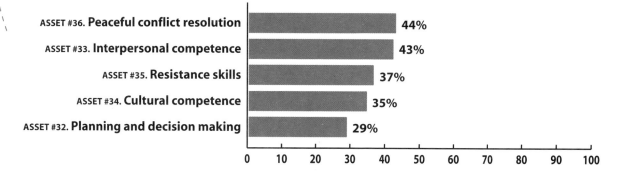

ASSET #36. **Peaceful conflict resolution** — 44%
ASSET #33. **Interpersonal competence** — 43%
ASSET #35. **Resistance skills** — 37%
ASSET #34. **Cultural competence** — 35%
ASSET #32. **Planning and decision making** — 29%

0 10 20 30 40 50 60 70 80 90 100

Building Social Competencies

Here are a few ideas for building the five social-competencies assets for children and youth at different ages. We've left spaces for you to jot down other ideas you think of or hear about.

Birth to Age 5

- Encourage young children to experiment with sounds.
- Give toddlers and preschoolers at least two equally appealing choices whenever possible.
- Allow young children to express their feelings, but give them guidelines on appropriate and inappropriate ways to act on their feelings.
- Continue to cheer on children's new skills.
- Encourage families to start having periodic family meetings where preschoolers have a voice in decision making.

- _____
  _____
- _____
  _____

Ages 6 to 11

- Emphasize that it is important for children to be able to use words, rather than actions, to express their needs and feelings.
- Encourage children to develop more skills in areas in which they are interested.
- Expose children to a variety of social situations, model appropriate behavior, and talk about what's acceptable and what's not.

- _____
  _____
- _____
  _____

Ages 12 to 18

- Help young people practice coping skills when difficult situations arise.
- Be gentle and supportive in responding to young people's fluctuating emotions.
- Give teenagers more chances to make decisions at home, at school, and in organizations. Coach them through the things they might weigh in coming to a decision.
- Ask teenagers about their dreams and help them with planning for the future.
- Teenagers: Seek out opportunities to mix with people from cultural/racial/ethnic backgrounds different from yours. Also, read books and see movies that give you exposure to diverse people, customs, and beliefs.

- _____
  _____
- _____
  _____

Your Skill Builders

W ho built your social-competencies assets during your childhood and/or adolescence? Was it someone in your family, a neighbor, a friend, someone at school, or a number of people working together? Below each social-competencies asset listed, write the name of each person (or people) who has nurtured that asset in you.

How did these people build your social-competencies assets?

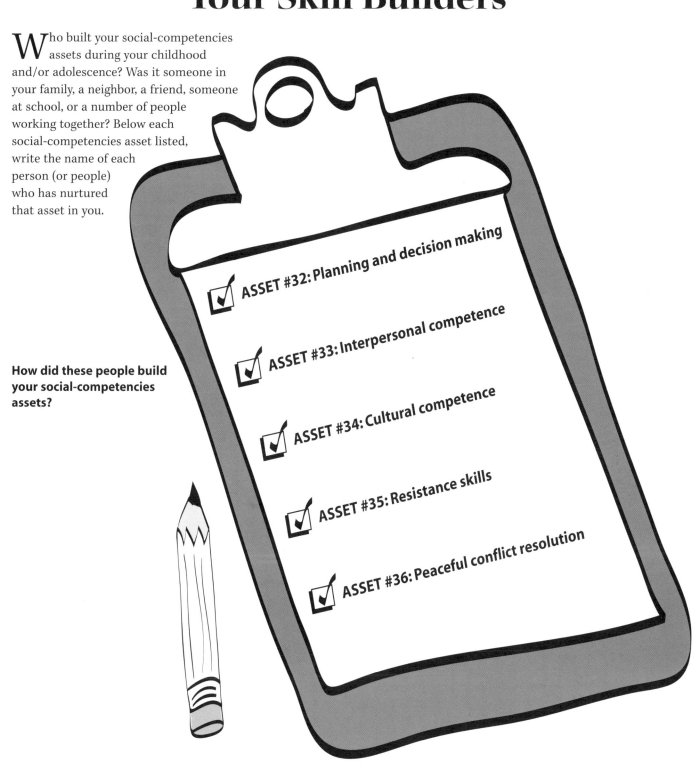

ASSET #32: Planning and decision making

ASSET #33: Interpersonal competence

ASSET #34: Cultural competence

ASSET #35: Resistance skills

ASSET #36: Peaceful conflict resolution

Ways to Build Social Competencies

No doubt you'll have many ideas of ways to build social competencies as you think about asset building in your life. Here are a few that others have tried and found helpful. We've also left some places for you to write in ideas that come to you.

Where You Live

- Celebrate cultural customs and rituals from your own heritage. Share those customs with neighbors, teammates, friends, and classmates by inviting them over for a meal that highlights food from your ethnic heritage.
- Dream about something you've always wanted to do. Using planning and decision-making skills, begin to create a plan that will make your dream a reality.

- _____
  _____
- _____
  _____

In an Organization

- Create opportunities for young people to build cultural competence by planning and/or celebrating cultural customs in creative ways.
- Think about ways you can involve young people in your organization's planning and decision-making agendas.

- _____
  _____
- _____
  _____

In Your Neighborhood

- For neighborhood block parties, have adults plan part of the party and young people plan another part.
- Invite over neighbors, especially children and teenagers. Get to know each person and share part of your interests so that neighbors get to know you.

- _____
  _____
- _____
  _____

Developing Critical Thinking Skills

Strengthening critical-thinking skills (the ability to think, plan, and evaluate) is a good way to build many of the social competencies. Critical thinking involves logic and creativity. Here are some steps to developing critical-thinking skills.

Step 1: Slow down your thinking and reaction. One of the hallmarks of critical thinking skills is taking time to think. Our society highly values people who can think quickly and think on their feet, but few people can do this well. Critical thinkers take the time to think.

Step 2: Expand your thinking skills. The best critical thinking involves using a number of different types of thinking skills. It may include making a list of pros and cons. Or, a critical thinker will look at a situation from a different angle.

Step 3: Ask others about your thinking strengths and weaknesses. People we know and trust often have helpful insights about which of our thinking skills are strong and which ones need more emphasis. Some people are more logical in their thinking while others find it easier to think creatively. Continue using the thinking skills that come easily to you, but be aware of different thinking skills and take time to explore and develop the ones that are harder for you.

Step 4: Take a workshop. Find a workshop that teaches planning, problem solving, decision making, or creative thinking. Community education centers often have one-time workshops on these subjects, and they can be fun and helpful.

Step 5: Use your critical thinking skills all the time. We all have critical thinking skills, and we just need to put them to practice. The more we use them, the more skilled we become with the five social-competencies assets.

Circles of Influence

Author Stephen Covey talks about people's "circle of influence." He contends that there are certain areas of our life where we have influence and other areas where we don't. He encourages people to focus energy on making a difference in the areas where they have influence.

When it comes to building social competencies, we have more influence than we think. In fact, we have a lot of influence.

Think about each of the social-competencies assets. How are you nurturing each one for others or for yourself? Who is included in your "circle of influence" for nurturing this asset? Consider others in your neighborhood or organization. How are they building each asset? Who is included in their "circles of influence"?

> **"You cannot shake hands with a clenched fist."**
>
> Indira Gandhi
> first female prime minister of India

ASSET #32
Planning and decision making

ASSET #33
Interpersonal competence

ASSET #36
Peaceful conflict resolution

ASSET #34
Cultural competence

ASSET #35
Resistance skills

Everyday Asset Building

Steve Unger is a facilities coordinator for the Upper Peninsula Children's Museum in Marquette, Michigan. He believes that young people can have fun while building social skills.

On the weekend, he likes to go sailing as a way to get away from it all. But he doesn't go alone; he brings young people with him. "It gives them one more thing they've done that's not drug- or sex-related, that's just plain fun," he says. Young people who go sailing with Unger become part of his crew, and each learns new sailing skills. "I'm not afraid to discuss life issues," he says about his time out on the water with the young people. "Kids like that." ✍

Having Your Say

A first step in helping young people build their social-competencies assets is to recognize your own strengths and challenges. Think about how well you already do with the five social-competencies assets. Rate your own social competencies on a scale of 1 (not well at all) to 5 (very well). Underneath each asset, jot down one or two things you'll start doing to nurture it.

Asset #32. Planning and decision making. How well do you plan ahead and make good choices?

Not well at all   1   2   3   4   5   Very well

Idea for building this asset:

Asset #33. Interpersonal competence. How well have you developed empathy, sensitivity, and friendship skills?

Not well at all   1   2   3   4   5   Very well

Idea for building this asset:

Asset #34. Cultural competence. How well do you interact with people of different cultural/racial/ethnic backgrounds?

Not well at all   1   2   3   4   5   Very well

Idea for building this asset:

Asset #35. Resistance skills. How well do you resist pressure to do things you believe are inappropriate or wrong?

Not well at all   1   2   3   4   5   Very well

Idea for building this asset:

Asset #36. Peaceful conflict resolution. How well do you resolve conflicts?

Not well at all   1   2   3   4   5   Very well

Idea for building this asset:

Having practical skills is important for young people to become well-rounded, confident young people. Building social-competencies assets takes teaching, our time, and our persistence. Young people don't develop skills overnight. They need time to learn them and time to practice them.

What three things would you say about the process of building social-competencies assets? What do you wish had been said to you when you were younger? Write one thing in each talk bubble.

When you have a chance, share your thoughts with a young person you know.

CHAPTER 9

Power, Purpose, and Promise

Twelve-year-old Aja Henderson of Baton Rouge, Louisiana, noticed that a lot of her friends and other children in the neighborhood didn't have anyone to take them to the library. Many parents worked, and the libraries were closed when the parents got home from work.

So, Aja decided to start her own library—in the den of her home. She started by stocking her library with her old books and then asked for donations from other people in her neighborhood. "At first the library was just intended for kids," she says. "But eventually grown-ups started coming, too."

Today Aja's library has 3,000 titles in it, and it's open seven days a week. She doesn't have any set hours because she wants people to be able to use it when it's convenient for them. Sometimes people stop by before she goes to school, and some come late in the evening.

Aja doesn't think what she has done is anything out of the ordinary. "I'm just a normal American kid," she says. "If I can do something like this, so can other kids. It just takes a little work and some creativity."

Aja's work to create a library also takes a strong, positive identity. This is what the last four of the 40 developmental assets are all about. When young people sense their own power, purpose, worth, and promise, they can do just about anything they decide to do.

The positive-identity assets tie in closely with the support assets. Young people who feel loved, supported, and nurtured are more apt to feel good about themselves and have a positive view of their future. Children and youth who have families, neighbors, friends, educators, and community residents who see the best in them are more likely to bring out the best in themselves and in those around them.

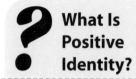

? What Is Positive Identity?

Young people need a strong sense of their own power, purpose, worth, and promise.

The Four Positive-Identity Assets

37 **Personal power**—Young person feels he or she has control over "things that happen to me."

38 **Self-esteem**—Young person reports having a high self-esteem.

39 **Sense of purpose**—Young person reports that "my life has a purpose."

40 **Positive view of personal future**—Young person is optimistic about her or his personal future.

How Young People Experience the Positive-Identity Assets

Young People Who Overcome the Odds

Much research has been done on young people who grow up in poverty, in abusive families, or with a parent with a severe mental illness. Researcher Norman Garmezy has found that those who become healthy, competent adults have a number of similarities, such as:

- Self-confidence.
- Optimistic persistence when facing frustration and failure.
- Ability to recover quickly from hard times and upsets.
- Winning personality that draws people to them.
- Easygoing nature.

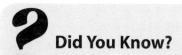

Did You Know?

- Boys are much more likely than girls to report having asset #38 (self-esteem) and asset #39 (sense of purpose).
- Asset #40 (positive view of personal future) is the asset most young people report having.

While some of these factors are part of a young person's temperament and personality, others are shaped as they grow by the people around them.

The Positive-Identity Assets: How They Stack Up

The four positive-identity assets indicate how young people feel about who they are and who they are becoming. Based on Search Institute surveys of almost 100,000 young people in 213 communities, the following percentages of young people report having these assets:

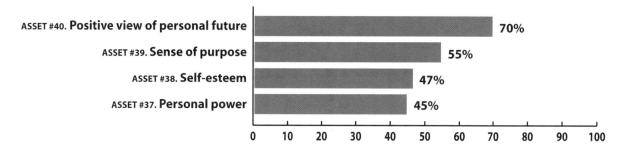

ASSET #40. **Positive view of personal future** 70%
ASSET #39. **Sense of purpose** 55%
ASSET #38. **Self-esteem** 47%
ASSET #37. **Personal power** 45%

0 10 20 30 40 50 60 70 80 90 100

Fostering a Positive Identity

Here are a few ideas for building the four positive-identity assets for children and youth at different ages. We've left spaces for you to jot down other ideas you think of or hear about.

Birth to Age 5

- Love, accept, and respect babies and young children unconditionally.
- Play together in ways that make young children laugh and enjoy the time together.
- Dwell on what children do right instead of what they do wrong. When a toddler or preschooler does make mistakes, focus on the behavior without making the child feel shame.
- Break new tasks and skills into small, manageable steps that preschoolers can master without becoming too frustrated.
- Encourage preschoolers to take pride in their cultural heritage and special talents.
- _____
  _____
- _____
  _____
  _____

Ages 6 to 11

- Help children seek out answers and solutions when they face difficult times.
- Encourage children to identify inspirational, positive role models to emulate.
- Play songs that talk about values. Read books together and look at what kind of personal power the characters have.

- Tell children that you'll love them no matter how wild they act, what grades they make, or how mad they get.
- Point out to a child her or his special talents, abilities, and strengths. Some children are amazing at solving puzzles or word-find games. Others can make something beautiful out of sticks and glue. Another can jump incredibly high. Notice these things and comment on them.
- _____
  _____
- _____
  _____

Ages 12 to 18

- Expect young people to experience ups and downs of self-esteem during these years, but expect self-esteem to increase as they get older.
- Avoid comparing young people with other young people.
- Have pride and take pleasure in teenagers' talents, capabilities, and discoveries. Share your pride.
- Support teenagers as they explore and struggle with issues of meaning, purpose, and vocation. Think with them about schooling after high school, career choices, life relationships, and values.

Nurturing Your Identity

We continue shaping our identities all of our lives. And sometimes the very areas where we need to focus energy are areas where we can help young people grow as well.

In each of the bubbles below, write one way that someone helped to nurture your own positive-identity assets when you were younger. How do you nurture each asset in yourself today?

Then look at the ideas again. How could you share some of these same ideas to strengthen young people's positive-identity assets? Star your best ideas.

ASSET #37. Personal power

ASSET #38. Self-esteem

ASSET #39. Sense of purpose

ASSET #40. Positive view of personal future

EXPLORING IDEAS

Ways to Build a Positive Identity

No doubt you'll have many ideas of ways to build a positive identity as you think about asset building in your life. Here are a few that others have tried and found helpful. We've also left some places for you to write in ideas that come to you.

Where You Live

- Make where you live a supportive, nurturing environment where people feel valued and loved for who they are. If you live alone, periodically invite others over to this warm, welcoming place.
- Delight in each family member's personality and unique interests and tastes. Be this way with people in your neighborhood and others you see.
- Talk about the things that give your life a sense of purpose. Ask others what gives their life purpose.
- When people where you live face difficulties, help them think through and act on solutions.

- _____
  _____
- _____
  _____

In Your Neighborhood

- Create a network that keeps track of everyone in the neighborhood. Cheer on and encourage neighbors who are doing well, and support those who are struggling.

- Start a short neighborhood newsletter to share stories and triumphs of neighbors of all ages.
- Leave messages (with chalk on sidewalks or by hanging notes on doors) saying how much you appreciate a certain neighbor. Do this for neighbors of all ages.

- _____
  _____
- _____
  _____

In an Organization

- Feature brief biographies of young people in your organizational newsletter. These can be young people who participate or children of employees.
- Sponsor a workshop, class, or event on one of the four positive-identity assets to encourage parents, adults, and young people to build a positive identity.

- _____
  _____
- _____
  _____

Becoming a Realistic Optimist

Some people are born with a capacity to see a positive angle on things. Others see the down side first. Building a positive identity includes blending healthy, optimistic attitudes that help us see and reach our potential with an understanding of the realistic steps needed to accomplish what we want or need. Here are some steps to becoming a realistic optimist.

Step 1: Understand what optimism is. In *The Optimistic Child,* author Martin E. P. Seligman reviewed 20 years of research on the subject to come up with this definition: "The basis of optimism does not lie in positive phrases or images of victory, but in the way you think about causes." He says that each person has a personality trait he calls an "explanatory style" that describes how we usually view why good and bad events happen to us.

Step 2: Learn more about your style. Seligman points out three parts of the explanatory style:

- **Permanence**—This refers to how we interpret the lasting power of things that happen. For example, optimists see negative situations as temporary and use words such as "sometimes" and "lately" to describe the difficult spot they're in. Pessimists see negative situations as permanent and use the words "always" and "never."
- **Pervasiveness**—This refers to our views on how a bad or good situation affects us. Seligman contends that optimists view good events as global and bad events as just specific points in time. For example, if optimists get a good grade on a math test, they'll say "I'm smart," whereas if they get a poor grade, they'll say, "I didn't study enough for that math test." Pessimists are the opposite. They view good events as specific and bad events as global. For example, if pessimists get a good grade on a math test, they'll say "I'm smart only in math," whereas if they get a poor grade, they'll say "I'll never get a good grade in any subject."
- **Personalization**—This refers to our view on who is to blame. Pessimists tend to blame themselves and optimists tend to blame the circumstance or other people. However, Seligman says that optimists also need to learn to have a balanced view of problems and take responsibility for their behaviors.

Step 3: Use your optimism to take action. Use this information to build your own positive-identity assets and those of children and young people you know. Work at becoming a realistic optimist.

Signs of Power, Purpose, Promise

All around us are signs of people using their power for good, people living out their sense of purpose, and people doing things that show promise and hope for the future. Think about people you know and about your community: Where do you see those signs? List examples of each on the signs below:

> *"I often dream about the day when every single youth in this world will be able to lift their heads way, way, way up high and say, 'I believe in myself.'"*
>
> Laura Garcia, 17

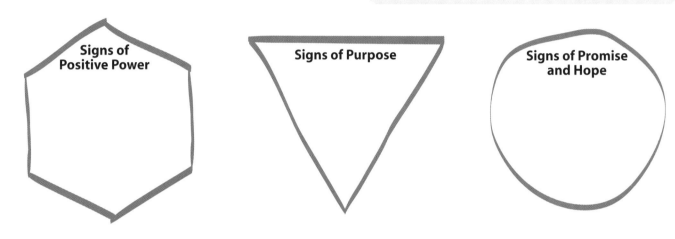

Signs of
Positive Power

Signs of Purpose

Signs of Promise
and Hope

How do these signs make you feel about your community? (Does it boost your "community esteem"?)

What can you do to affirm and support these signs of power, purpose, and promise?

Everyday Asset Building

Paul Miller, an engineer, happened to find out that his 12-year-old neighbor, Anna Navarro, was interested in science when she asked Miller if he would help her out with a science fair project.

Miller had no idea that helping Navarro would lead to mentoring her for six years and that Navarro would end up going to international competition and making a presentation before Nobel laureates. By the time

Navarro had completed six award-winning projects, Miller and his wife, Felicia, had converted their basement into a science lab and their kitchen into a strategy room.

"If I had known up front what I was getting into, I might have been afraid of doing it," Miller admits. "But when you see what a child can do, it's worth it."

Make a Wish

A s you look around your neighborhood or organization, do you sense that most people are optimistic or pessimistic? If you were to make one wish about young people having the positive-identity assets, what would you wish? Write your wish inside the wishbone, along with one way you can help make the wish come true.

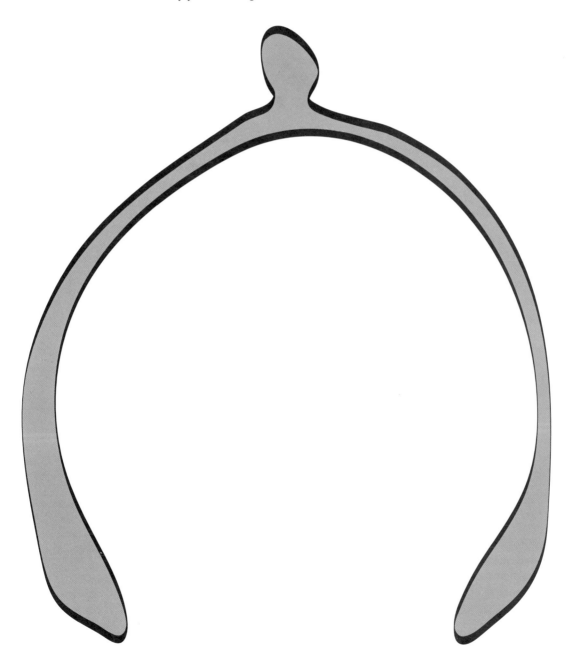

CHAPTER 10

Asset Building: Taking the Next Step

Being an asset builder is an approach to life, a philosophy we can incorporate into our roles as neighbor, student, parent, employee, mentor, or volunteer. It's a role we all have—and one we all share. It's a role we need to take seriously.

How can you be a successful asset builder? Look at the word *assets* itself. Each letter of the word can represent an important action step.

Act—Start now. Asset building isn't just about talking. It's about doing something. Choose one small thing you can do immediately and start today. Do something every day—even if it's small, something as simple as smiling at every young person you see.

Seek support—Build small, caring communities of adults and young people who believe in asset building. Get to know each other. Talk about the issues you face. Share ideas. Teach each other. Support each other.

Stretch yourself—How else can you build assets? While it's best to start small and do what's easy, it's also important to challenge yourself to do more. How can you make asset building a way of life? How will it change your life, too?

Expand what you know—Learn more about asset building. Meet more children and young people. Get to know more of your neighbors. Find out what they hope for and what their dreams are for themselves and for young people. Find out more about your community and how residents can build assets.

Tell others—Spread the word about assets and asset building. Begin by linking up with like-minded people. But don't stop there. Find ways to reach out to various individuals and organizations throughout your community so that everyone is building assets.

Stick with it—Asset building works when we make a long-term commitment to bringing out the best in young people. We need to build assets over and over again—and with as many young people as we can.

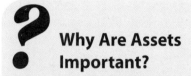

Why Are Assets Important?

They reduce high-risk behaviors. The more assets young people have, the less likely they are to get involved in alcohol use, violence, skipping school, and other high-risk behaviors.

They increase helpful behaviors. The more assets young people have, the more likely they are to be leaders, succeed in school, overcome adversity, and take care of their health.

They work. The more assets young people have, the more likely they are to grow up healthy and become competent, caring adults.

The Challenge:

The average young person has 18 of the 40 developmental assets. How can we increase and build assets for and with all young people?

The Power and Promise of Assets

How the 40 Assets Stack Up, Grade by Grade

While the average young person has 18 assets, the average number of assets varies slightly depending on how old the young person is. Based on Search Institute surveys of almost 100,000 young people in 213 communities, the following percentages show the average number of assets of young people over the years.

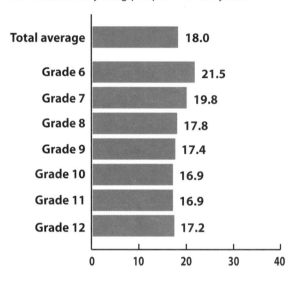

Total average	18.0
Grade 6	21.5
Grade 7	19.8
Grade 8	17.8
Grade 9	17.4
Grade 10	16.9
Grade 11	16.9
Grade 12	17.2

Six Key Principles of Asset Building

1 All children and youth need assets.

2 Everyone can build assets.

3 Asset building is an ongoing process.

4 Relationships are key.

5 Delivering consistent messages is crucial.

6 Duplication and repetition are necessary.

Everyday Asset Building

Al Ernest of Newark, Ohio, could have decided a long time ago that he was done with interacting with young people. His three daughters had all left home and were in college.

He worked in a manufacturing plant, and he could have spent his time investing in his career and hobbies. But not Al. Today he continues to be a Scout leader. He mentors a 5th-grade boy each week for an hour at the local public school.

And he's created an asset-building program at his workplace.

Because of Al, hourly employees at Owens Corning can take a paid hour off each week to be a mentor at a nearby elementary school. Employees also volunteer to help out at school events.

"The value of asset building is that it puts the job we have to do into bite-size pieces," Al says. And Al continues to do his bit, piece by piece.

EXPLORING IDEAS

Ways to Keep Building Assets

Here are a few ideas for building assets for children and youth at different ages. We've left spaces for you to jot down other ideas you think of or hear about.

Where You Live

- Make asset building a part of your daily life. Each day, be intentional about building assets for and with at least one young person in your neighborhood and for and with everyone who lives in your household.
- Examine each household member's assets. Which 10 assets does each person think are her or his strongest? weakest? Talk about how you can build all the assets.
- Ask the people you live with how they like to be supported. If you live alone, ask your closest friends or family members. Support each other in those ways.
- Link with other households that are interested in building assets. Swap ideas.

- _____
  _____
- _____
  _____

In Your Neighborhood

- Find other neighbors who want to make a long-term commitment to asset building. Begin developing strategies for building assets within your neighborhood.
- Discuss people's asset-building vision for the neighborhood. What do you want your neighborhood to be like in 3 years? 5

years? 10 years? How can young people help to shape and then work toward that vision?
- Get the word out about asset building to neighbors who aren't familiar with asset building or who don't seem interested. Figure out ways to get them on board.

- _____
  _____
- _____
  _____

In an Organization

- Create an asset-building team of individuals interested in making asset building a part of your organizational life.
- Examine your organization's role in your community. What does it have to offer young people that no other organization can? How can it build assets?
- Network with other organizations in your community to find ones interested in asset building. See how much more you can do together than you could ever do alone.

- _____
  _____
- _____
  _____

The Young People You Touch

Use this page to help you think about the young people in your life.

1. Think about 1 to 3 young people who are particularly important to you—special friends, your children, your grandchildren, someone you mentor, or others. Write their names in the palm of the hand.

2. Then think of 5 to 10 other young people whose lives you touch, even if only a little. It may be at work, at school, on your block, in your apartment complex, in your congregation, where you shop, through your volunteer efforts, or other settings. Write their names in the fingers of the hand.

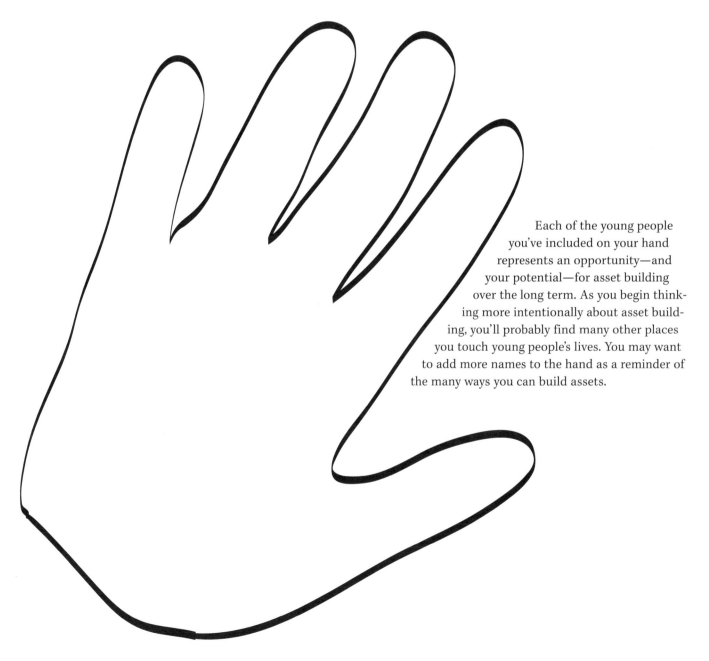

Each of the young people you've included on your hand represents an opportunity—and your potential—for asset building over the long term. As you begin thinking more intentionally about asset building, you'll probably find many other places you touch young people's lives. You may want to add more names to the hand as a reminder of the many ways you can build assets.

LOOKING FORWARD

What's Your Piece?

This chapter stresses how you can make a difference as an asset builder. When each person builds assets, we can create an interlocking web of support for young people.

What one thing can you do to build assets? What is your unique piece? Write it on the puzzle piece.

An important thing about puzzles is that puzzle pieces only make sense when they're linked with other pieces. On each of the four joints on the puzzle, write one place or person you can link to for asset building with children and teenagers.

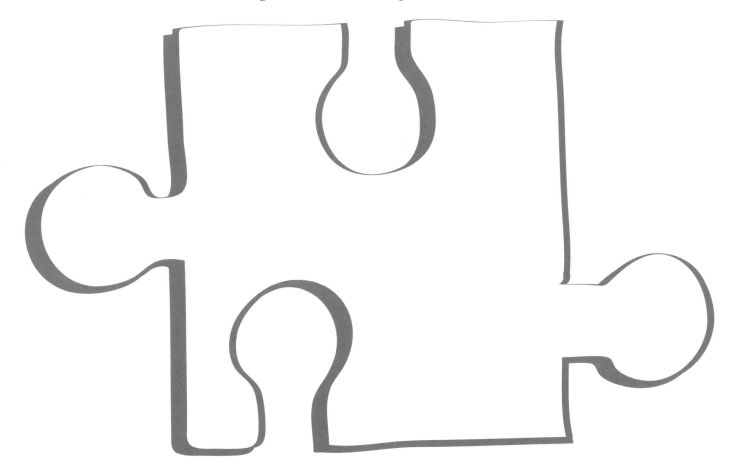

> *"A hundred years from now it will not matter what my bank account was, the sort of house I lived in, or the kind of car I drove. But the world may be different because I was important in the life of a child."*
>
> Kathy Davis
> in *Helping Kids Succeed—Alaska Style*

Resources to Explore

Chapter 1

If you're interested in more in-depth information on the developmental assets and where they came from, you may want to examine some other resources from Search Institute. For more information on these and other asset-building resources, contact Search Institute, 700 South Third Street, Suite 210, Minneapolis, MN 55415. Toll-free: 800-888-7828. Web: www.search-institute.org

All Kids Are Our Kids is the groundbreaking, in-depth book by Search Institute president Peter L. Benson, Ph.D., that gives detailed information on the assets and how communities can mobilize individuals and organizations to build assets in young people.

Assets: The Magazine of Ideas for Healthy Communities and Healthy Youth offers information and strategies for building assets and promoting positive youth development.

Introducing Healthy Communities · Healthy Youth is an informational handout that provides an overview of the Healthy Communities · Healthy Youth initiative and Search Institute. It opens to a colorful poster of asset-building ideas.

Starting Out Right: Developmental Assets for Children offers new frameworks for understanding and building the foundation that children from birth through age 11 need to begin a healthy life.

What Kids Need to Succeed is an easy-to-read book that gives practical ideas for building each developmental asset.

What Teens Need to Succeed is a comprehensive, practical book that describes specific ways young people can build each of the 40 assets for themselves and others.

Chapter 2

Asset #1. Family Support
Parenting with a Purpose by Dean Feldmeyer and Eugene C. Roehlkepartain (Minneapolis, MN: Search Institute, 1995) explains how to build support while building assets for and with your child.

Wonderful Ways to Love a Child and *Wonderful Ways to Love a Teen* both by Judy Ford (Berkeley, CA: Fine Communications 1997) give inspiring, practical ideas on providing support.

Asset #2. Positive Family Communication
The 7 Habits of Highly Effective Families by Stephen Covey (New York: Golden Books, 1997) is a 390-page book filled with stories and ideas on how to communicate more effectively as a family.

Positive Self-Talk for Children by Douglas Bloch (New York: Bantam Books, 1993) is a step-by-step guide on how to speak more positively to children while also teaching them how to speak in a more positive way to themselves.

Asset #3. Other Adult Relationships
Contemporary Grandparenting by Arthur Kornhaber, M.D. (Thousand Oaks, CA: Sage Publications, 1996) provides powerful, practical ways on how to support and care for a teenager so that the relationship is mutually satisfying.

Asset #4. Caring Neighborhood
101 Things You Can Do for Our Children's Future by Richard Louv (New York: Anchor Books, 1993) includes a chapter on what you can do in your neighborhood.

Asset #5. Caring School Climate
Learning and Living: Integrating Asset Building into a School's Mission by Dr. Donald Draayer and Eugene C. Roehlkepartain (Minneapolis, MN: Search Institute, 1998) suggests ways to create an asset-building climate in your school.

Asset #6. Parent Involvement in Schooling
Parents Are Powerful compiled by Anne T. Henderson (Washington, DC: Center for Law and Education, Community Action for Public Schools, 1996) is a practical guide on how to be involved in a child's education from elementary school through high school.

The U.S. Department of Education offers a number of free publications on family involvement in learning. Call 800-USA-LEARN.

Chapter 3

Asset #7. Community Values Youth
Empowering Your Child by C. Fred Bateman (Norfolk, VA: Hampton Roads Publishing, 1990) suggests how to create an empowering environment where you live and how to be an empowering parent.

Creating Community Anywhere by Carolyn R. Shaffer and Kristin Anundsen (New York: Putnam, 1996) describes practical ways to build community and roles for children.

Asset #8. Youth as Resources
Releasing the Imagination by Maxine Greene (San Francisco: Jossey-Bass, 1995) stresses the importance of engaging young people in critical thinking and taking action to have a positive impact on their communities.

Kidstories by Jim Delisle (Minneapolis, MN: Free Spirit Publishing, 1991) profiles real kids who are doing things to improve themselves, their schools, their communities, or their world.

Asset #9. Service to Others
Kid's Guide to Service Projects: Over 500 Service Ideas for Young People Who Want to Make a Difference by Barbara A. Lewis (Minneapolis, MN: Free Spirit Publishing, 1995) includes simple projects and long-term commitments.

50 Simple Things You Can Do to Save the Earth by the Earthworks Group (Berkeley, CA: Earthworks Press, 1989) suggests a variety of ways to serve others through environmental projects.

Asset #10. Safety
Safe Homes, Safe Neighborhoods by Stephanie Mann (Berkeley, CA: Nolo Press, 1993) is a practical guide about how to create a sense of safety in your home and neighborhood.

The Gift of Fear by Gavin De Becker (Boston: Little, Brown & Co., 1997) explains how to recognize true signs of safety and danger while suggesting ways to expand your intuitive sense.

Chapter 4

Asset #11. Family Boundaries
Positive Discipline by Jane Nelsen (New York: Bantam, 1996) is the classic guide on setting boundaries and responding to specific behaviors while helping young people become responsible, cooperative, and self-disciplined. Nelsen also has written other discipline books for specific needs. Each of these books is published by Prima Publishing in Rocklin, California, and they include: *Positive Discipline for Single Parents* (1993), *Positive Discipline for Blended Families* (1997), *Positive Discipline for Preschoolers* (1998), and *Positive Discipline for Teenagers* (1994).

Parenting Toward Solutions by Linda Metcalf (Englewood Cliffs, NJ: Prentice Hall, 1997) suggests how to create and enforce family boundaries in positive, effective ways.

Asset #12. School Boundaries
A Parent's Guide to Innovative Education by Anne Wescott Dodd (Chicago, IL: Noble Press, 1992) offers positive strategies for how adults and young people can bring out the best in their schools.

Asset #13. Neighborhood Boundaries
The Neighborhood Works (Chicago, IL: Center for Neighborhood and Technology) is a magazine that publishes articles on creating effective neighborhoods that have boundaries and caring neighbors.

Waging Peace in Our Schools by Linda Lantieri and Janet Patti (Boston: Beacon Press, 1996) explores an approach to keeping violence out of school based on the Resolving Conflict Creatively Program in use in hundreds of schools across the country.

Asset #14. Adult Role Models
Heroes: Shaping Lives through Family and Culture by Steffen Kraehmer (Minneapolis, MN: Fairview Press, 1995) is a practical handbook for helping young people find positive heroes in their lives.

Asset #15. Positive Peer Influence
Positive Peer Groups by Sharon Scott (Minneapolis, MN: Johnson Institute, 1988) suggests how young people can work together to solve their own challenges and make their world even better.

Asset #16. High Expectations
Awakening Your Child's Natural Genius by Thomas Armstrong (New York: Jeremy P. Tarcher, 1991) suggests creative ways to enhance young people's learning abilities, curiosity, and creativity.

Chapter 5

Asset #17. Creative Activities
Growing Up Creative: Nurturing a Lifetime of Creativity by Teresa Amabile (Buffalo, NY: Crown, 1989) gives practical, helpful tips on how to develop a child's creativity.

Raising a Creative Child by Cynthia MacGregor (New York: Carol Publishing Group, 1996) has creative and meaningful activities to do with children from ages 3 to 15.

Asset #18. Youth Programs
1998-1999 Directory of American Youth Organizations by Judith B. Erickson (Minneapolis, MN: Free Spirit Publishing, 1998) is a comprehensive guide of 500 youth programs including clubs, groups, troops, teams, societies, and more.

Making the Case by Nancy Leffert and others (Minneapolis, MN: Search Institute, 1995) shows how a wide range of youth development programs build assets and contribute to young people's healthy development.

Asset #19. Religious Community
Building Assets in Congregations: A Practical Guide for Helping Youth Grow Up Healthy by Eugene C. Roehlkepartain (Minneapolis, MN: Search Institute, 1998) is a comprehensive book that gives concrete suggestions for creating an asset-building congregation.

Something More: Nurturing Your Child's Spiritual Growth by Jean Grasso Fitzpatrick (New York: Viking Penguin, 1991) helps parents of all faiths deepen spirituality in family life in everyday ways.

Asset #20. Time at Home
Ideas for Families by Phyllis Pellman Good and Merle Good (Intercourse, PA: Good Books, 1992) lists ideas on how to enjoy your time together as a family.

New Games for the Whole Family by Dale N. LeFevre (New York: Perigree Books, 1988) suggests fun, easy-to-do activities for families of all ages.

Chapter 6

Asset #21. Achievement Motivation
365 Ways to Help Your Child Learn and Achieve by Cheri Fuller (Colorado Springs, CO: NAVpress, 1994) lists creative ways to help young people feel motivated to learn more.

The Parents' and Teachers' Guide to Helping Young Children Learn edited by Betty Farber, M. Ed. (Cutchogue, NY: Preschool Publications, 1997) gives practical ways to help young children learn, using ideas from 35 respected experts in the field.

Asset #22. School Engagement
The Growth of the Mind by Stanley I. Greenspan (Reading, MA: Addison-Wesley, 1997) stresses that intelligence is more than being smart; it also hinges on morality, empathy, and self-reflection.

Your Child's Growing Mind by Jane M. Healy (New York: Doubleday, 1987) helps you guide children's learning from birth through the teen years.

Asset #23. Homework
Homework Improvement by Roberta Schneiderman (Glenview, IL: GoodYearBooks, 1996) is a parent's guide to helping young people develop lifelong, successful study habits.

Asset #24. Bonding to School
Boxed In and Bored by Peter C. Scales (Minneapolis, MN: Search Institute, 1996) is a report that examines how middle schools often fail young people and what good middle schools do right.

Asset #25. Reading for Pleasure
The Mother-Daughter Book Club by Shireen Dodson (New York: HarperCollins, 1997) shows how parent-child book clubs can build this asset while also deepening the bond between parents and their children and building community with others.

The Read-Aloud Handbook by Jim Trelease (New York: Penguin Books, 1995) gives practical ways on how to teach young people to love reading so that they continue reading.

Read All about It! by Jim Trelease (New York: Penguin Books, 1993) is a collection of stories, poems, and newspaper articles to read aloud with young people and pique their interest in the featured writers and their other works.

International Reading Association (800 Barksdale Road, P.O. Box 8139, Newark, DE 19714-8139; 800-336-READ) offers a number of brochures and books that promote reading.

Chapter 7

Positive Values Assets (in General)
What Do You Stand For? by Barbara A. Lewis (Minneapolis, MN: Free Spirit Publishing, 1998) invites young people to explore and practice their values.

Teaching Your Children Values by Linda and Richard Eyre (New York: Simon & Schuster, 1993) gives age-appropriate ideas on how to help children develop values.

Asset #26. Caring
Teaching Your Kids to Care by Deborah Spaide (New York: Citadel Press, 1995) includes 105 creative caring activities for children in kindergarten through grade 12. It also suggests practical ways to develop a caring spirit in children.

Asset #27. Equality and Social Justice
The Kid's Guide to Social Action by Barbara A. Lewis (Minneapolis, MN: Free Spirit Publishing, 1998) is the revised and expanded version of the book that gives step-by-step instructions on how young people can make a difference in the world.

Asset #28. Integrity
Integrity by Stephen L. Carter (New York: Basic Books, 1996) gives an in-depth look at why integrity is important.

Asset #29. Honesty
The First Honest Book about Lies by Jonni Kincher (Minneapolis, MN: Free Spirit Publishing, 1992) encourages readers from age 13 and up to develop honesty as a personal value.

Asset #30. Responsibility
Raising a Responsible Child by Elizabeth M. Ellis (New York: Birch Lane Press, 1995) suggests how to deal with overindulgent behavior so that young people develop responsibility.

Asset #31. Restraint
Flight of the Stork by Anne C. Bernstein (Indianapolis, IN: Perspectives Press, 1994) explains what kids understand about sex and reproduction at each age and how to encourage them to develop restraint.

Parenting for Prevention by David Wilmes (Minneapolis, MN: Johnson Institute, 1996) focuses on how to raise children to say no to alcohol and drugs.

Chapter 8

Social Competencies in General
Common Sense Parenting by Ray Burke, Ph.D., and Ron Herron (Boys Town, NE: Boys Town Press, 1996) suggests practical ways to build a variety of social competencies in young people.

Asset #32. Planning and Decision Making
The Life-Smart Kid: Teaching Your Child to Use Good Judgment in Every Situation by Lawrence J. Greene (Rocklin, CA: Prima Publishing, 1995) gives practical ways to help young people develop decision-making skills.

Asset #33. Interpersonal Competence
Emotional Intelligence by Daniel Goleman (New York: Bantam, 1995) makes the case that people with self-awareness, impulse control, persistence, zeal, self-motivation, empathy, and social deftness are more likely to succeed.

Asset #34. Cultural Competence
40 Ways to Raise a Nonracist Child by Barbara Mathias (New York: HarperCollins, 1996) gives practical, age-specific advice (from infancy through the high school years) on how to teach young people to shun prejudice.

Asset #35. Resistance Skills
Helping Kids Learn Refusal Skills by David Wilmes (Minneapolis, MN: Johnson Institute, 1991) is a booklet that gives practical advice on how to help kids develop resistance skills.

Asset #36. Peaceful Conflict Resolution
Raising a Thinking Child by Myrna B. Shure (New York: Pocket Books, 1996) presents a variety of techniques for teaching children up to age 7 how to solve their problems creatively and nonviolently.

Peace Patrol by Eden Steele (Spring Valley: Inner Choice Publishing, 1994) lays out step-by-step peaceful conflict-resolution skills for young people to use.

Chapter 9

Asset #37. Personal Power
Stick Up for Yourself! by Gershen Kaufman (Minneapolis, MN: Free Spirit Publishing, is a book written for teenagers that gives practical ways to have personal power and a positive self-esteem.

Asset #38. Self-Esteem
The Winning Family by Louise Hart (Berkeley, CA: Celestial Arts, 1996) suggests how parents can increase self-esteem in their children and themselves.

Full Esteem Ahead: 100 Ways to Build Self-Esteem in Children and Adults by Diane Loomans (Tiburon, CA: H. J. Kramer, 1994) gives many creative ways to build self-esteem in people of all ages.

Feeling Great by Terry Orlick, Ph.D. (Carp, Ontario: Creative Bound Inc., 1996) emphasizes children's total development and has more than 100 fun-filled activities to do as a family.

Asset #39. Sense of Purpose
Kids Who Make a Difference by Joyce Roche (Portland, OR: MasterMedia Publishing, shows young people from all ethnic, economic, and geographic backgrounds who found a sense of purpose and did extraordinary things.

Do What You Love, the Money Will Follow by Marsha Sinetar (New York: Dell Publishing, 1989) wrestles with the question of finding meaningful work that fits your sense of purpose.

Find Your Calling, Love Your Life by Martha Finney and Deborah Dasch (New York: Simon & Schuster, 1998). An exploration of how to find a sense of purpose in life and work that is true to your self.

Asset #40. Positive View of Personal Future
The Optimistic Child by Martin E. P. Seligman, Ph.D. (Boston: Houghton Mifflin, gives step-by-step advice on how to safeguard young people from depression while helping them master optimism.

Helpful Web Sites

http://www.search-institute.org
This Web site includes many ideas of how individuals, organizations, neighborhoods, and communities can build assets. It also has information about more than 250 communities across the nation involved in asset building.

http://www.coolbeanz.com
This Web site for young people includes a section about how young people can build assets. (See the "Get Serious" portion of this Web page.)

http://www.kidscampaign.org
Published by the Benton Foundation, this Web site does not mention the concept of asset building, but its message of child advocacy fits well with asset building. It has practical ideas on how you can support young people.